Patrick T. Terenzini
The Pennsylvania State University
EDITOR-IN-CHIEF

Ellen Earle Chaffee
North Dakota University System
ASSOCIATE EDITOR

Pursuit of Quality in Higher Education: Case Studies in Total Quality Management

Deborah J. Teeter
The University of Kansas

G. Gregory Lozier
The Pennsylvania State University

EDITORS

Number 78, Summer 1993

JOSSEY-BASS PUBLISHERS
San Francisco

PURSUIT OF QUALITY IN HIGHER EDUCATION: CASE STUDIES IN TOTAL QUALITY MANAGEMENT
Deborah J. Teeter, G. Gregory Lozier (eds.)
New Directions for Institutional Research, no. 78
Volume XV, Number 2
Patrick T. Terenzini, Editor-in-Chief
Ellen Earle Chaffee, Associate Editor

Microfilm copies of issues and articles are available in 16mm and 35mm, as well as microfiche in 105mm, through University Microfilms Inc., 300 North Zeeb Road, Ann Arbor, Michigan 48106.

LC 85-645339   ISSN 0271-0579   ISBN 1-55542-693-X

NEW DIRECTIONS FOR INSTITUTIONAL RESEARCH is part of The Jossey-Bass Higher and Adult Education Series and is published quarterly by Jossey-Bass Inc., Publishers, 350 Sansome Street, San Francisco, California 94104-1310 (publication number USPS 098-830). Second-class postage paid at San Francisco, California, and at additional mailing offices. POST-MASTER: Send address changes to New Directions for Institutional Research, Jossey-Bass Inc., Publishers, 350 Sansome Street, San Francisco, California 94104-1310.

SUBSCRIPTIONS for 1993 cost $45.00 for individuals and $60.00 for institutions, agencies, and libraries.

EDITORIAL CORRESPONDENCE should be sent to the editor-in-chief, Patrick T. Terenzini, Center for the Study of Higher Education, The Pennsylvania State University, 403 South Allen Street, Suite 104, University Park, Pennsylvania 16801-5202.

Photograph of the library by Michael Graves at San Juan Capistrano by Chad Slattery © 1984. All rights reserved.

 The paper used in this journal is acid-free and meets the strictest guidelines in the United States for recycled paper (50 percent recycled waste, including 10 percent post-consumer waste). Manufactured in the United States of America.

For information about the Association for Institutional Research, write to the following address:

AIR Executive Office
314 Stone Building
Florida State University
Tallahassee, FL 32306-3038

(904) 644-4470

CONTENTS

New Directions for Institutional Research, no. 78, Summer 1993 © Jossey-Bass Publishers

INTRODUCTION

Over time, higher education has seen numerous management fads come and go. Accordingly, we should not be surprised that faculty and staff are suspicious of a management philosophy that proclaims its aims as boldly as Total Quality Management (TQM) does.

In spite of such suspicion, there is growing evidence that the principles and concepts of TQM have much to offer higher education. This volume is dedicated to exploring the application of TQM to institutions of higher education and builds on the New Directions for Institutional Research volume *Total Quality Management in Higher Education* (Sherr and Teeter, 1991), which focused on the concepts and principles of TQM.

To provide the reader with glimpses of the many facets and aspects that TQM can assume in a variety of institutional settings, this volume, *Pursuit of Quality in Higher Education: Case Studies in Total Quality Management*, assembles over twenty vignettes. These vignettes are grouped into four sections: Part One, Concepts and Culture, discusses the undergirding philosophy that permits an organization to deal with cultural issues and ultimately leads it to a total cultural transformation. The first chapter reviews the foundations of TQM so that readers who are not familiar with it have a context for understanding and interpreting the vignettes that follow. Part Two, Continuous Improvement Results, recounts experiences on many campuses demonstrating that the pursuit of TQM principles can produce improvements in the classroom, help to refocus and reorganize academic units, improve staff attitudes, and reduce costs. Part Three, Methods, Tools, and Techniques, describes experiences with a number of tools and mechanisms that aid process improvement. And Part Four, Organizing for Total Quality Management, shares experiences indicating that the pursuit of TQM involves much more than the learning of concepts and tools. Stories of successes and failures provide the knowledge necessary for improvement. In the concluding chapter, we review the findings of studies reporting on the failures of TQM in corporate settings and summarize some of the pitfalls to avoid.

A matrix summarizing the characteristics of the institutions represented in this volume and the status of TQM at these institutions is presented in the Appendix. The reader may find it helpful to review this information first as a context for the vignettes.

The literature on TQM is extensive. Some of this literature is cited in chapters of this volume, most notably, *Out of the Crisis* (Deming, 1986) and *The Fifth Discipline: The Art and Practice of the Learning Organization* (Senge, 1990). Moreover, the body of literature about TQM and higher education is growing. We recommend *Total Quality Management in Higher Education*

(Sherr and Teeter, 1991), which contains an extensive annotated bibliography on TQM literature. *Transforming Higher Education* (Chaffee and Sherr, 1992), and *On Q: Causing Quality in Higher Education* (Seymour, 1991).

Deborah J. Teeter
G. Gregory Lozier
Editors

References

Chaffee, E. E., and Sherr, L. A. *Transforming Higher Education.* ASHE-ERIC Higher Education Reports, no. 3. Washington, D.C.: Association for the Study of Higher Education, 1992.

Deming, W. E. *Out of the Crisis.* Cambridge: Center for Advanced Engineering Study, Massachusetts Institute of Technology, 1986.

Senge, P. M. *The Fifth Discipline: The Art and Practice of the Learning Organization.* New York: Doubleday, 1990.

Seymour, D. *On Q: Causing Quality in Higher Education.* Washington, D.C.: American Council on Education, 1991.

Sherr, L. A., and Teeter, D. J. (eds.). *Total Quality Management in Higher Education.* New Directions for Institutional Research, no. 71. San Francisco: Jossey-Bass, 1991.

DEBORAH J. TEETER is director of institutional research and planning at The University of Kansas, Lawrence.

G. GREGORY LOZIER is executive director of planning and analysis and a member of the graduate faculty in higher education at The Pennsylvania State University.

PART ONE

Concepts and Culture

*Understanding the underlying principles of Total Quality
Management is a necessary foundation for pursuing quality.*

Six Foundations of
Total Quality Management

G. Gregory Lozier, Deborah J. Teeter

Ask anyone how to define *quality,* and he or she is likely to use the following
types of descriptors: reliability, affordability, performance, timeliness,
value, style of presentation, anticipating needs, and accommodating wants.
The three leading proponents of Total Quality Management (TQM) offer
these definitions:

Quality is "fitness for use" (Juran, 1989, p. C3)
Quality is "conforming to requirements" (Crosby, 1984, p. 59)
Quality is "surpassing customer needs and expectations" (Deming, in
    Gitlow and Gitlow, 1987, p. 35).

People everywhere increasingly expect products purchased and services received to embody these characteristics. Global competitiveness
heightens the attention to and concern about quality. However, few are
willing to define quality in colleges and universities, although many claim
that they know intrinsically when it is present. Similarly, faculty and
administrators alike are reluctant to call a student or anyone else a *customer.*
This environment presents strong objections to the language, principles,
and methods of TQM.
    But consider the following:

Should students expect to graduate in four years?
Should students be able to tell a faculty member that material in last
    Wednesday's class was unclear?

NEW DIRECTIONS FOR INSTITUTIONAL RESEARCH, no. 78, Summer 1993   © Jossey-Bass Publishers

What is a reasonable time period for being reimbursed for university travel (perhaps before the credit card statement arrives)?

Are finals needed if teaching-learning feedback is provided throughout the term?

Should students have to go to five different offices to withdraw from a course?

Does a requisition for a $15 laboratory supplies purchase really need three signatures?

Answers to these questions and to concerns about the applicability of TQM to higher education raise such issues as these: expectations, human interrelationships, understanding of the ways in which work gets done, trust or the lack thereof, and the cost in increased complexity that results from abuse by a few.

Colleges and universities interested in improving their responses to these questions are facing change, important change, in the way they look and think about themselves and the way they function. This change focuses on the pursuit of quality. In many respects, the principles of TQM are neither new nor unique. What is new is the recognition that we can and must pursue quality consciously by systematic means. The remainder of this chapter discusses six foundations of TQM for colleges and universities.

Establishing a Mission: Focus on the Customer

Understanding and improving quality requires knowing what we do, our purpose as an organization. The first of Deming's (1982) fourteen points for management is to "create constancy of purpose." Constancy of purpose requires patience and a long-term commitment to a well-established and well-understood mission statement that provides the organization with a framework for making decisions in a consistent manner. Gitlow and Gitlow (1987, p. 19) observe that "the process of (1) developing a mission statement, (2) making it a living document, and (3) socializing new employees to the mission statement is what is needed to begin the 'journey to quality.'" Commitment to purpose provides the motivation for long-term change.

According to Collins and Porras (1991, pp. 38, 41), a statement of purpose also conveys "how the organization fills basic human needs . . . and plays an essential role in determining who's inside and who's outside the organization." A purpose or mission statement identifies not only what the organization does but also the individuals or groups—the customers— whom it serves. Knowing who receives the benefits of teaching, research, and service becomes a requisite to quality enhancement. Referring to the three definitions of quality cited earlier, mission should specify whose use, whose requirements, and whose needs and expectations.

Through our primary functions and the full array of supporting services, colleges and universities serve a broad range of customers, both within and without the institution: employees, students, parents, government officials, business and industry, alumni, and funding agencies. Focusing on the needs of customers requires us to learn what those needs are, oftentimes to distinguish needs from wants, then to meet and exceed the associated expectations. Critics of the applicability of TQM principles and concepts to higher education often say that *customer* is an inappropriate term. Yet, should employees not expect the payroll office to process payroll checks accurately? Should students not expect to be able to register for the courses required for their major? Should presidents not expect accurate enrollment reports? Should students seated in the third row and beyond not expect to see class transparencies?

Creating a Vision

If mission is knowing the answer to what an organization does and for whom it does it, vision tells us where the organization is going. A vision statement describes what the organization will be like when its mission and goals are achieved. The vision declares what the organization wants to become. It can mean doing more or being different, but it most certainly should mean being better. Without a vision, the college, university, or individual unit within the institution interested in the pursuit of quality is likely to spin its wheels without advancing or improving.

Improving the Process Continuously

Processes—the flow of work activities—are the means by which we carry out our mission. We pay much attention to *inputs* (for example, the test scores of entering students, the number of Ph.D. faculty members, the number of books in the library, or the budget of the university), *design* (for example, curricula, research proposals, information systems design), and *output* (for example, the number of graduates, the number of graduates employed, and the scores of graduates on national tests). We pay far less attention to the means we use to deliver and support instruction, research, and service. These means include academic processes, academic support processes, and administrative support processes. For example, the following processes take place at most colleges and universities: teaching and learning, grant proposals, research investigation, library book circulation, grade processing, student admission, curriculum development, advising, orientation, registration, testing and evaluation, payroll, purchasing, and faculty recruitment.

Pursuing quality through TQM requires eliminating or reducing mistakes in all these and other processes. There are three types of process mistakes: rework, scrap, and unnecessary complexity. *Rework* is work spent fixing earlier mistakes. It means taking a course over again, repeating material not adequately covered in a course prerequisite, redrafting a check originally issued in the wrong amount, or reprinting a publication that contained incorrect information. *Scrap* is work that is discarded and begun over again. It means faculty terminations and aborted faculty searches, flunked students, ignored committee recommendations, and abandoned planning processes. *Unnecessary complexity* involves steps that add no value to the process. It means too many signatures on a change-of-major form, endless steps in a course approval process, five different forms to apply for admission, and elaborate justifications for the purchase of equipment. All of the examples just given of rework, scrap, and unnecessary complexity could be characterized as process defects. Ultimately, process improvement comes not from detecting these defects—for example, through testing at the end of a course to determine whether a student knows the subject matter—but from preventing such defects, for example, by using systematic analysis to determine whether the subject matter is being adequately presented (taught) and received (learned).

Using Systematic Analysis

"In God we trust; all others must use data." This remark, usually attributed to Deming, conveys the importance of data and analysis for the pursuit of quality. Total Quality Management has its roots in statistical quality control (SQC). SQC began with the agricultural experiments of the British statistician R. A. Fisher in the early part of this century, and in the 1930s it was applied to manufacturing by W. A. Shewhart at American Telephone and Telegraph's Bell Laboratories. Organizations now use statistics increasingly to model processes and determine ways of improving both process and output. Thus, TQM places considerable emphasis on the scientific method, or what Shewhart termed the *plan-do-check-act (PDCA) cycle* (Sherr and Lozier, 1991, p. 8):

Plan: Identify a process in need of improvement, analyze the problems, and develop a proposal for change that will cause some type of improvement.

Do: Run an experiment with the proposed change.

Check: Collect data to determine whether the experiment produced the desired change.

Act: If the experiment is successful, implement the idea more broadly; if not, learn from the mistake and try an alternative.

In addition to being systematic, the scientific method also requires us to base changes on fact rather than on conjecture or intuition. Several fundamental but relatively unsophisticated statistical tools can help understand processes and analyze data about processes. These tools include flowcharts, cause-and-effect diagrams, Pareto charts, checklists, histograms, scatter diagrams, and run and control charts. The purposes of collecting data and analyzing it statistically are to identify where variation exists in a process and what causes it.

Understanding the role of variation is fundamental to the pursuit of quality and systematic analysis. Variation exists in every process. There are two types of variation: special causes and common causes. *Special causes* arise from unique circumstances; they are not part of normal functioning. Special causes create abnormal variation or surprises in the process. The first step in process improvement is to eliminate special causes. The faculty member who does not cover all the expected material in a prerequisite course, an electrical outage that shuts down the information system during registration, or an influenza outbreak in the financial aid clerical pool the week before aid awards are announced are examples of special causes in higher education that can disturb a process and alter its intended effects. The ability to improve a process requires elimination of these special causes.

Common causes are inherent in the process, occur regularly over time, affect everyone working in the process, and affect all outcomes of the process. Many such causes create rework, scrap, and unnecessary complexity. The second step in process improvement is to identify and reduce variation from common causes through careful, data-based, permanent changes in the process. Reducing the time required for physical plant repairs could mean carrying the parts most often needed on the repair truck rather than withdrawing them from general stores each time they are needed. Improved training for personnel directing new employees how to complete the employment form could reduce errors in payroll. If data indicate that completing homework assignments enhances learning, measures to promote doing homework could reduce the number of students who flunk.

A process without special causes is "in control," that is, it is stable and predictable. Once a process is in control, quality-improvement-based steps can be undertaken to reduce the variation arising from common causes.

Promoting Participation

Teamwork and team decision making are important aspects of quality process improvement. To improve processes requires teams of people, whether these teams are confined to an organizational unit or they represent several cross-functional units. These teams must understand the process, and they must be committed to its improvement.

Participation requires empowerment—an atmosphere in which people feel comfortable, confident, motivated, and responsible for conducting their work. Members of a team share responsibility and credit for the team's decisions and accomplishments. Participation recognizes that the people most intimately involved in a process understand best how it functions and how to improve it. Participation also focuses on the way in which things get done, not on blaming workers for failures or defects.

When 80 percent of the students cannot clearly see the experiment being demonstrated, it does not improve quality to tell students not to miss the laboratory class. Exhorting employees to work faster will not shorten the time required to process student registrations. Providing too few sections of a required course will not increase student satisfaction with advising. Unless we involve the participants, we are unlikely to understand a process well enough to improve it.

Higher education lags significantly behind the corporate sector in its attention to ongoing human resource training and development. Yet, colleges and universities are in the business of education, and their functions are human resource intensive. Quality improvement requires that people know how to do their jobs—how to advise, how to teach, how to do research, how to process a form, and how to handle telephone inquiries. They need to know how their job relates to the jobs that others do and how their functions contribute to the mission.

In a quality organization, teamwork becomes standard operating procedure, and employee participation becomes part of the organizational culture. Use of teams is one means of promoting participation. Structured teams can be instrumental in helping individuals understand the principles of focusing on the customer, systematic analysis, and continuous improvement.

At some colleges and universities, teams have examined such particular processes as physical plant renovations, disposition of hazardous waste, recovery of sponsored research funding, processing of financial pledges, faculty hiring, freshman orientation and advising, human resource office telephone response time, and the learning of physics by engineering students. However, if special teams are the only means by which the organization pursues quality, the prospect of achieving continuous improvement is greatly diminished. According to Scholtes and others (1988), special teams can become dysfunctional if they communicate that quality improvement is a separate function outside one's normal work relationships and responsibilities. In a transformed organization, the pursuit of quality is a way of life that is not limited to activities associated with special teams.

Recognizing the University as a System

The next step after teamwork is systems thinking. Senge (1990) calls this the *fifth discipline* and says that it serves as the foundation of the learning organization. According to Senge (1990, p. 13), "A learning organization is a place where people are continually discovering how they create their reality." The learning organization constantly expands its capacity to create the future by recognizing that the success of any individual depends on the success of others.

With respect to the pursuit of quality and TQM, systems thinking reinforces the need to recognize the interrelationships among the people, processes, and subunits of an organization. Systems thinking tells us that we cannot improve the learning process unless we work with the students who are doing the learning; we cannot improve purchasing response time without involving the departments making the purchases; we cannot improve information systems without interviewing those who use the systems hardware and software. It tells us that teaching faculty who have a high instructional load contribute to the success of faculty who conduct cutting-edge, funded research and teach less.

Conclusion

These foundations for the pursuit of quality can have a powerful impact on efforts to improve higher education. The vignettes that follow exemplify these foundations.

References

Collins, J. C., and Porras, J. I. "Organizational Vision and Visionary Organizations." *California Management Review,* 1991, *34* (1), 30–51.

Crosby, P. B. *Quality Without Tears.* New York: McGraw-Hill, 1984.

Deming, W. E. *Quality, Productivity, and Competitive Position.* Cambridge: Center for Advanced Engineering Study, Massachusetts Institute of Technology, 1982.

Gitlow, H. S., and Gitlow, S. J. *The Deming Guide to Quality and Competitive Position.* Englewood Cliffs, N.J.: Prentice Hall, 1987.

Juran, J. M. *Juran on Leadership for Quality: An Executive Handbook.* New York: Free Press, 1989.

Scholtes, P. R., and others. *The Team Handbook: How to Improve Quality with Teams.* Madison, Wisc.: Joiner, 1988.

Senge, P. M. *The Fifth Discipline: The Art and Practice of the Learning Organization.* New York: Doubleday, 1990.

Sherr, L. A., and Lozier, G. G. "Total Quality Management in Higher Education." In L. A. Sherr and D. J. Teeter (eds.), *Total Quality Management in Higher Education.* New Directions for Institutional Research, no. 71. San Francisco: Jossey-Bass, 1991.

G. GREGORY LOZIER is executive director of planning and analysis and a member of the graduate faculty in higher education at The Pennsylvania State University.

DEBORAH J. TEETER is director of institutional research and planning at The University of Kansas, Lawrence.

The introduction of Total Quality Management can create a new awareness of class distinctions among employees and a new demand for respect, dignity, and equity—essential characteristics of a quality organization.

Classism and Quality

Robert L. Carothers, Mary Lou Sevigny

The centennial anniversary of the founding of the University of Rhode Island (URI) created an opportunity for the university to look back with pride on one hundred years of service and forward to an ever more productive, though economically constrained, future. During this period of reflection, we introduced the principles of Total Quality Management (TQM) to our campuses. The discussion of what it meant to be customer driven or to have empowered employees operating in self-managing teams generated both heat and light at URI, but among the most significant and painful revelations was the unrecognized importance of the class structure at the university.

Historically, strategic planning at the university was largely top down, and the university community often focused on the tension between the administration and the faculty in this process. This pattern reemerged as the new president set forth a vision for the university's second century, and the faculty began to weigh in with various degrees of enthusiasm and doubt. The president appointed a joint academic steering committee composed of deans and faculty members to facilitate debate and discussion on the proposal and to devise a strategy for moving forward. The new vision included operating the university consistent with the principles of TQM. As members of the university community began to understand the philosophy of quality and its emphasis on participation and empowerment, it became clear that the vast majority of the people employed by the university were not represented at the steering committee table. But now the faculty, having secured some parity with the administration, hesitated to set additional places. In response to voices pointing up this inconsistency, the president appointed a parallel committee for the university's two thousand staff employees, the University Staff Steering Committee (USSC).

NEW DIRECTIONS FOR INSTITUTIONAL RESEARCH, no. 78, Summer 1993 © Jossey-Bass Publishers

13

The nineteen members of the USSC quickly charted a different course. Their first formal action was to rewrite their charge, focusing on how staff could better serve the university. Four critical questions framed the work to be accomplished: How can we improve service to our customers or constituencies as a university? How can we improve service to our customers or constituencies by improving service between departments and divisions of the university? How can we improve service to our customers or constituencies by improving our relationships with each other? How can we improve service to our customers or constituencies by improving the development of individuals? The committee developed and refined each of these key questions. For example, a subset of the fourth question was, How do we reward a person who, year after year, accepts new challenges and continually redefines his or her role in serving the university? To seek the answers, members of the USSC sought aggressively to engage their associates.

Over the next two months, the USSC distributed surveys to all employees with their paychecks and held two sets of open forums. While many staff members came to the forums and spoke eloquently of their concerns, attendance by faculty and students was minimal, and hope that these various customer groups would give their input through this process faded. The committee turned next to focus groups, a decision that ultimately proved to be the most important one that the committee would make. Over the next three weeks, the committee held thirty-eight focus groups involving more than five hundred staff, students, and faculty.

From these sessions emerged a new understanding of the role of class in the dynamics of our university. For example, one committee member described the committee itself as unique with respect to its function: "The committee found itself entrusted with confidential information, and it absorbed the frustration and anger felt by the community." It became, she said, the spokesperson—the voice or the agent—for the community, and the community became the author of the final report.

The USSC report, a forty-page document printed and distributed throughout the community, identified fourteen key challenges, issues, and opportunities for the university's future. Treatment of staff personnel and the prevalent "class system" perception headed the list. The report identified a number of common perceptions to describe the treatment issue. For example, the skills, capabilities, and perspectives of frontline staff are often not recognized and used to the advantage of the university. The university community is deficient in showing respect for staff employees as individuals and for the contribution that they make to the university. Staff are concerned about the presence of racism, sexism, and paternalism in the workplace of the university. Similar factors described the "class system." For example, staff, including student employees, at various levels in the university organization sense the presence of a hierarchical "class" or "caste" structure that encourages discrimination on the basis of an individual's or group's position in the organization. There is also a perception that rules, regulations, and privileges are not consistently enforced or extended to individuals at different levels of the organizations.

The discussions uncovered many examples illustrating points made in the report. A departmental secretary reported being "uninvited" to a faculty-student reception because the presence of support staff at the function was deemed inappropriate. A technician indicated that her supervisor had never acknowledged her extra efforts and achievements in the lab but that she was routinely expected to remain after normal working hours to assist that supervisor. Janitors and crafts people spoke of being treated as children and of managers who seemed to assume that the staff were trying to get away with something. Staff are required to punch in and out on time cards, while faculty come and go without apparent constraints. "Does the university really trust us so much less?" one computer programmer asked.

The committee's principal findings contain some important lessons for our future and for the pursuit of TQM at the University of Rhode Island. For example, improving the manner in which the institution collectively recognizes, respects, and values people—their contributions, their skills, and their human dignity—may offer the greatest contribution to enhanced quality. Improving interpersonal relationships among members of the university community is key to improvements in service and in the quality of life at the university.

It is clear that those who understand the principles of TQM expect empowered employees to be treated with respect and their efforts at continuous improvement to be recognized. The experience of the University of Rhode Island reminds us all that TQM has an implicit ethic, an ethic of service and a commitment to human dignity. As one janitor told us, "All this sounds like the Golden Rule to me." She is right. Each of us should remember to serve as we would be served, to lead as we would be led. That is real quality.

ROBERT L. CAROTHERS is president of the University of Rhode Island, Providence.

MARY LOU SEVIGNY is lead computer analyst at the University of Rhode Island's administrative computing center and a member of the University Staff Steering Committee.

Opening up an institution to total quality management requires patience, openness, a commitment to new ideas, and a commitment to the customer.

Samford University's Quality Story

John W. Harris

How do we describe an incomplete voyage when there are no precise charts that allow us to gauge our progress toward our destination? Academics pursuing Total Quality Management (TQM) are drawn to it by visions of using all university operations to improve the effectiveness of learning and teaching. These individuals may qualify as paradigm pioneers (Barker, 1989), in which the decision to begin a TQM voyage springs more from belief and the heart than from data and rationality.

This chapter uses a question-and-answer format to present a collection of musings about aspects of the pursuit of quality, augmented by stories from Samford University's voyage into TQM.

"How Did You Sell Your President and Other Administrators on TQM?"

Actually, one cannot, or at least should not, sell TQM to anyone. Instead, one tries to increase understanding. While we tried to avoid selling, some surely feel that we persuaded them to accept TQM against their better judgment. I still occasionally hear administrators say in so many words, "Having this customer satisfaction stuff thrown at me so much gets tiresome." There are many times when administrators cannot give faculty or staff what they ask. All too often, the latter respond by saying, "You are not meeting my needs as a customer." But even getting faculty and administrators to consider the concept of student as customer begins with leadership.

Samford's president, Thomas Corts, was a leader ready for TQM to happen. His focus on students as customers is tied to his understanding of marketing in higher education: "At the heart of a consumerist approach in any service industry is an adaptation of an old rule: Perform your service as

New Directions for Institutional Research, no. 78, Summer 1993 © Jossey-Bass Publishers

if you were on the receiving point rather than the delivery point of the transaction. If teachers would teach as they would like to be taught, custodians cleaned as they would like their houses cleaned, questions were answered as we would want our own questions answered, the world would be happier, and the college would be a better place. In truth, marketing consciousness will have to be promoted (perhaps 'marketed') within the college community" (Kotler and Fox, 1985, p. 31).

TQM calls for profound change in most of us. For example, persuading administrators that they are not supervisors but facilitative leaders demands emotional as well as cognitive learning. It does not come easy to anyone, particularly to an administrator over fifty who reached a high position by doing what he was told and following institutional policies and procedures. The same is true of teachers. They find it very hard to move from dispensing information to facilitating student learning.

"What Strategies Did You Use to Entice Academics to Join You on This Voyage?"

While businesspeople may see TQM sooner or later as having an impact on the financial sheet, academics are more likely to get hooked on ideas. At Samford, we asked the president and provost to write papers about two aspects of TQM: customer orientation and servant leadership. As an authority on classical rhetoric, the president wrote that Aristotle advocated customer orientation when he urged speakers to take their hearers' perspective into account. The provost, a theologian, wrote about the Judeo-Christian view of the team leader as servant.

We demonstrated the president's and provost's commitment to TQM by widely circulating the papers on customer orientation and servant leadership. These papers proved that academics can link TQM concepts with their respective disciplines. Even more, they resonated with the Christian values that we at Samford hold. Focusing on the needs and interests of those served by one's work reflects the Golden Rule. The TQM concepts remind us of the values that we espouse but often do not practice in our work.

"How Did You Prepare for Your TQM Journey?"

Samford's leadership team spent one day or more every month for six months studying and discussing TQM. In the seventh month, we invited an external consultant to walk the team through an exercise on mission-customers-processes-values-vision (MCPVV). She introduced us to some of the quality planning tools, for example, affinity groups and spider diagrams. The team met from 7:45 A.M. to 12:00 noon every day for one week. By week's end, we had reams of butcher paper with phrases about MCPVV. It took us another fourteen months, another three days with our consultant, and yet another month to get our MCPVV in shape to distribute to all faculty and budget heads for comment. Now, a year later, every unit has an MCPVV that uses the university's MCPVV as a point of reference.

"Could You Have Implemented TQM with Less Pain and More Front-End Understanding?"

Maybe, but I doubt that there is any way of learning TQM abstractly while remaining safe and secure. At some point, one has to take the plunge.

For example, our English department chair reports that her department did not take writing its MCPVV very seriously the first time through. Later, while going through a national peer review, she and her colleagues looked back at their MCPVV. They decided the first document did not provide the direction and focus that they needed. They now send the rewritten MCPVV to prospective faculty members and refer to it in promotion and tenure decisions. Every unit uses its MCPVV in our new approaches to assessment, planning, and budgeting.

As a part of preparing for the TQM journey, Samford also committed to continual learning as an organization. Senge (1990) makes a compelling case that only organizations that learn will prosper or even survive in the twenty-first century. Who, especially academics, can argue about learning? Nevertheless, the idea that organizations learn breaks the paradigm of learning, even for academics. Perhaps more than any other group, academics think of learning as restricted to individuals. For some, group learning gets very close to cheating.

We believe that Senge's notion of learning organization comprehensively represents what we are after in TQM. For this reason, the president convened the quality council at his home on three evenings to discuss certain chapters of Senge's book. Again, we stressed getting the ideas or increasing understanding. Increasingly, we think of the university as a web of processes, and some day we may understand it as an integrated organism with complementary, mutually supporting functions.

"As a Learning Organization, What Kind of Training Do You Provide at Samford in Preparation for the TQM Journey?"

At Samford, training and orientation for TQM concentrate more on the basic ideas of TQM than on its techniques for two reasons: First, we need everyone at Samford to help translate TQM to the academy. We believe this is best done by starting with the basic ideas rather than with the techniques derived from them. Second, we started with the basic ideas to increase the appeal to faculty, since academics are trained to identify and critique the presuppositions behind any set of techniques.

"Whom do You Invite to the Orientation and Training Sessions? Any Special Concerns?"

Some advised us not to mix faculty and staff in TQM orientations since faculty would not take kindly to orientation and training with physical plant and accounting staff. Nevertheless, we mixed them. At the luncheon concluding each training series, one participant after another stated how much he or she had enjoyed getting to know other people doing different jobs.

I am now more aware than ever before of the class-consciousness of universities (see Carothers and Sevigny, this volume). Of all social institutions, we expect universities to be very egalitarian. I now fully appreciate how academic class consciousness works against TQM. A professor does not make the money of nonacademics with similar levels of education. Nevertheless, academics may comfort themselves by owning certain territory and credentials. Since the professors set the example of protecting turf and credentials, university staff often establish turf and credentials of their own. Yet, at the root, I believe, faculty and staff long to connect with others and with the larger purposes of the institution.

During the 1990–1991 academic year, we provided deans, middle-level administrators, and certain faculty and staff with twenty-three hours of TQM orientation. Again, we stressed ideas over hands-on training. In spring 1992, the president asked me to provide an orientation to TQM for everyone on campus. I scheduled 7:00 A.M. orientations on quality improvement (QI) for certain Thursday and Friday mornings between July and December 1992. The president invited every employee, faculty member, and staff member to these early morning orientations. For nonexempt employees, we counted these hours as part of their work time. We showed relevant videos, brought in local speakers, and arranged for QI teams to report on their work.

"After All of These Preparations, What Happened When You Launched TQM Teams?"

Examples of the impact of TQM on Samford abound. Several follow to provide a glimpse into the potential impact that TQM can have on organizations embracing these concepts.

Nursing Licensure. In February 1989, morale in the nursing school reached an unexpected low when only 45 percent of the Samford graduates sitting for the licensing examination passed. For the last four testings, the percentages of those passing have been 100 percent, 90 percent, 100 percent, and 100 percent, respectively. Working with the quality assessment office, the dean and her faculty began a long search for causes. Guesses abounded. One of the most popular was that the problem lay with the transfer students. However, an analysis of grades and test scores uncovered no significant difference between transfer and other students.

As Baur (this volume) reports, investigation revealed that the problems lay with control and alignment. First, we discovered that we were admitting unprepared students to the program. Second, much of the instruction and classroom testing emphasized note taking and memorization. In contrast, the new licensing examinations called for problem solving and de-emphasized facts. Moreover, we did not necessarily align courses with one another. Consequently, students did not reach the competencies required in subsequent courses.

Daily Work Life. To illustrate QI in daily work life, we can point to what happened when the director of residence life asked for a change in the no-refund policy for room rent. The old policy stated that a student who signed a semester lease assumed responsibility for fulfilling the lease. At the same time, we prorate refunds for tuition and board. The president asked about the financial implications of making the room rent policy consistent with the tuition and board refund policy. Less than $2,000 was at stake, so we changed the time-consuming, student-irritating policy.

Here is another illustration of the way in which QI can be incorporated into daily activities: To review problems with a choral conducting class, a teacher in the school of music asked students to use a cause-and-effect (fishbone) diagram to brainstorm the causes.

Teaching Quality. A new general education mathematics course includes the basic TQM statistical tools. A premedical student who took the course interviewed for a summer job at a hospital in her hometown. She learned that some of the hospital's quality teams needed help with the statistical tools and in her interview proclaimed, "I know that; I've just completed a course in it." She got the job. We hear that major companies are warning M.B.A. students that they will need to know TQM in order to be considered for hiring. We believe that many employers, not just those hiring M.B.A.'s and engineers, would like to hire graduates with experience in TQM.

Student Teams. As part of her doctoral dissertation, a graduate student designed and piloted a manual for student QI teams in conventional classes. The manual posits that students should act as coworkers with the teacher in producing their learning. The instructor invites three to five student volunteers to collect information from students in the class about what is and is not working. The feedback occurs early in the semester, which enables the faculty member to take corrective action while the course is in progress. Three teachers piloted the manual in three summer 1992 classes: accounting, biology, and mathematics. All three instructors and their students liked the procedure. More faculty tried it in about fifteen classes at Samford in fall 1992. Faculty at several other universities are now testing the concept. The provost envisions replacing the student teaching evaluation questionnaires that we distribute at the end of classes with student QI teams.

Library Reorganization. Several major events led to a deterioration in library staff morale. Plans called for doubling the library's space. An expert on information literacy spoke to faculty and library staff about how they could better serve the Samford community. At about this time, four librarians participated in the quality training that we provided for deans and middle managers of the university. When a professional librarian position was vacant, a planning committee discussed how the position might be filled. In summary, committee members used the TQM tools to redefine all positions, resigned from all current positions, reapplied for the new positions, and created a concentric, flatter organizational structure. As Thomason (this volume) describes, both service and morale increased.

Residence Hall Work Order. The physical plant staff examined their work order process for the residence halls. The old process required a student to complete a request form and send it to the resident assistant in the dorm. The resident assistant sent it to the central residence life office, which in turn sent it to physical plant. The team collected time series data from the point at which the student submitted the order to the time when physical plant received it. The old process required at least two days and in a few cases as many as seven. Now the student calls an answering service, which faxes the requests directly to physical plant in twelve hours or less.

"What Are the Impact and Effectiveness of the Cross-Functional Teams?"

We are less successful with cross-functional teams. A cross-functional team on energy conservation identified lighting as the primary consumer of energy on campus. After further study, the team proposed various technical adjustments that could save about $135,000 per year. The projected payback could pay for other energy conservation measures. The barrier to implementation was a one-year $475,000 retrofit. In a tight budget year, the cost was too great. We let the team down, and management was frustrated.

Other cross-functional teams experienced similar problems. A team working on recycling presented a solution requiring significant capital and personnel costs. A year after the recycling team made its report, we are beginning to act on its proposal. Both the energy and the recycling teams did outstanding work, but because we could not implement their recommendations immediately and completely, skepticism about the quality effort surfaced.

These teams did not cause the problem. The process for setting up cross-functional teams created the problem. We learned that cross-functional teams need well-defined missions and clear limits. Furthermore, they need to communicate their progress or lack of it regularly to their sponsor and the QI facilitator. We failed to advise these teams up front about the very limited funds. Moreover, when they moved into areas beyond budget capabilities, they needed to know that their solutions could not be funded.

Nevertheless, the cross-functional team scene is not all dark. The most important cross-functional team, the freshman year experience team, led to several major changes. Six individuals composed this team: vice president for student affairs (chair), dean of arts and sciences, dean of academic services, head of the biology department, campus minister, director of student activities, and director of the freshman forum. This team researched the basic literature on late adolescent and early adulthood development as well as student development in general. Next, it prepared an affinity diagram outlining the needs and expectations of students and what we should expect of them. On the basis of this work, it developed a survey for freshmen and their parents. The survey identified major concerns in both groups that resulted in two major changes: First, Freshman Forum, which had been required, was made totally voluntary, and course content was changed to respond to the needs of Samford students. Second, freshman orientation was given a more academic emphasis. The team continues to work after twenty-one months of operation.

The activities of the freshman year experience closely resemble quality function deployment (QFD). In industry, QFD is used to take customers' needs and expectations into account during the design and redesign phases of product development. I believe that QFD is a powerful tool for designing all academic programs and services. It requires going beyond designing a course or service, delivering it, and then surveying students for their evaluation. It means designing curricula and courses around the interests and needs of stakeholders, be they students, employers, graduate or professional schools, or professional licensing or certification groups. It most clearly does not mean designing courses to give the students good grades for the least amount of effort.

If we were starting over, I would resist having cross-functional teams until we gained considerable experience with workgroup teams. Some cross-functional teams worked on minor issues that did not justify the time and talent that were spent. I would limit cross-functional team members to those with prior workgroup experience or those with extensive training. And we would appoint cross-functional teams only for major tasks, give them clear missions, and suggest target dates.

"How Do You Empower Teams?"

Increasingly, we believe that we can act to improve the processes that we own. Recently, the dean of academic services simplified the process and forms for drop and add. The new director of human resources streamlined the procedure by which a person leaving Samford employment or retiring signs out. When a quality team made an interim report about a very convoluted process, the team leader said about a certain form, "I have never liked it!" The president asked her why she had never changed it. She obviously felt that she did not have the power to change it. The president encouraged her to do so as soon as possible.

Empowerment means more than giving people more authority. In some cases, empowerment leads people to think that they can do what they want. Somehow we need to get across that they are empowered to serve the needs and expectations of those who depend on their work. Empowerment also includes the discipline of understanding one's work, its flow and variations, so that one can deal with the sources of customer dissatisfaction.

"What Is the Role of Institutional Research in TQM?"

The dictum "In God we trust; all others must use data" is catching on. We have fewer discussions at which we only exchange opinions. Administrators expose more data about budgets and budget choices. We use more data about functions, but we still lack critical data on cross-functional processes. For example, we need information about every step in the enrolling process. Our factbook of the future should report performance measures on every one of the eight cross-functional processes, for example, learning, living, and staffing.

"How Do You Identify Opportunities for Improvement?"

Besides having units identify areas for improvement, two suggestion systems operate at Samford: Opportunity to Improve Samford (OTIS) and Sound Off About Samford (SO-AS). OTIS is designed to elicit substantive proposals for process improvements. Through SO-AS, anyone can gripe without proposing a solution. We started OTIS in fall 1990 and added SO-AS about a year later. An analysis of the OTIS program after two years revealed that most proposals deal with administrative rather than academic concerns. Our goal is to respond to the OTIS suggestions within one month's time, but many take much longer. We found that the responding unit often explains, sometimes defensively, rather than examines its current positions.

Nevertheless, these suggestion systems are responsible for several changes that might not otherwise have occurred. For example, physical plant put shelves in women's rest rooms because of an OTIS suggestion. A suggestion from a student in the interior design program resulted in the provost allocating $66,000 to speech, art, and music for a joint computer lab.

We began by having OTIS suggestions sent to a presidential assistant who functioned as an ombudsman. He decided whether to give the suggestions to the provost or to another vice president, who in turn sent it on to the appropriate unit for a response. When the answer came back, the ombudsman communicated the response to the person or persons who originated the suggestions.

When the ombudsman retired, the president's assistant for management and budget began to handle proposals. He suggested to the provost and vice presidents that he route OTIS and SO-AS proposals directly to the appropriate units, and they agreed. Given the more direct routing and the fact that this assistant works much more closely with the actual operations of the university, suggestions moved faster.

We learned several lessons. First, suggestion programs unearth real problems that often escape notice. Second, one can expect slow response to suggestions early in a quality improvement program. Fear is still high, and various groups are just learning to work together. Furthermore, at this stage the persons in charge want to be in the loop. Third, it is much easier to defend the current policy than it is to take time to understand the suggestion and think seriously about changing the policy. Fourth, the president needs to balance responsiveness to customers and empowerment of academic and support function administrators. Fifth, the fact that a suggestion transcends several functional areas does not always justify the creation of a cross-functional team. Such teams eat up valuable time and dissipate enthusiasm for tackling the big problems when opportunities arise. They deserve process problems worthy of their time and talents. While there is a downside to starting a suggestion program in the early stages of TQM, it remains a viable way of addressing concrete customer concerns.

"After Embarking on the TQM Journey, What Changes Did You Make in the Organization to Stay the Course?"

Samford is small (fall 1992 headcount: 4,341; full-time equivalents: 3,977), and its religious orientation gives it a common purpose. Nevertheless, members of the university community still need to learn to work together toward that purpose. To improve the university's organizational and functional alignment and attain greater constancy of purpose (Deming's initial principle of continuous improvement), we took the following steps:

1. Over a period of fourteen months, the quality council developed a MCPVV statement with the help of a consultant skilled in the use of executive planning tools.
2. The quality council shared the university MCPVV with all faculty and administrators and requested suggestions for improvement.
3. The council used this input to revise the university MCPVV.
4. Each academic department and support unit constructed its own MCPVV consistent with the university MCPVV.
5. The president appointed an assessment, planning, and budgeting panel (AP&B) composed of a diagonal cross-section of faculty and staff.
6. The AP&B panel and quality council provided feedback to the provost and each vice president on the alignment of his respective unit's MCPVV. The provost and each vice president interpreted these comments to their

respective units. The provost asked the eight school deans to comment on all eight MCPVVs.

7. All departments and units are developing methods to ask their customers to evaluate the fulfillment of their mission, the effectiveness of their *processes*, their consistency with their *values*, and their movement toward their *vision*.

8. The AP&B panel and the quality council commented on the assessment plans of each department and unit.

As a result of this alignment effort, our language about the purpose of the university is more consistent, and we think more about those whom we serve. The shorthand version of our mission comes easily to mind: "Samford's mission is to nurture persons—faculty and staff as well as students."

What have we learned from this effort? First, we still find it easier to write to each other than to interact face to face. This exercise consumed many hours and reams of paper. Second, because the process involves paper, we tend to focus more on the wording of the MCPVV than on daily behavior. Some of our most effective and most service-oriented units did not produce outstanding MCPVVs. More important, we want to use the exercises as opportunities to stimulate dialogues that allow groups access to "a larger 'pool of common meaning' which cannot be accessed individually" (Senge, 1990, pp. 240–241). While we believe that this is happening, we continue to look for more efficient ways of encouraging dialogue across campus.

Moreover, we are still conventionally organized around the vertical functions of academics, student affairs, business affairs, university relations, and athletics. More important, we still function in these vertical stovepipes. We have not named a provost for learning or a vice president for living or enrolling—three examples of our eight cross-functional processes.

Deming (1986) lays the quality organization on its side; he shows it as a system of lateral processes. We are beginning to understand that this must happen, but how do we do it without debilitating trauma? Our library staff showed the courage to change their organization from one of hierarchical boxes to a flatter, concentric, mutually reinforcing model. By all comparisons, administrators ought to know more about management organization than librarians do. Barker (1989) shows that those who know the most about the rule of the current paradigm find it almost impossible to see the new one. He attributes the breakthroughs of Alex Mueller, a Nobel prize–winning physicist, and Fred Smith, founder of Federal Express, to their operational naivete.

The way we organize formally is not nearly as important as the way we work. We now work together more across our structure of hierarchical boundaries. Nevertheless, staff, who lack the protection usually afforded academics, are particularly careful about venturing across boundaries.

When Deming says that we must learn to work together, we may think he just means being nice to one another. However, I believe that he is calling for structural changes. In any case, a university cannot optimize its resources so as to meet and exceed student needs until everyone works together. Too much emphasis on who reports to whom certainly gets in the way.

"Has Samford Achieved Any Significant Organizational Breakthroughs as a Result of TQM?"

Major breakthroughs rarely occur until several years into a journey. We probably expected too much too soon, but we did achieve a major breakthrough in that our mission statement avoids the railroad fallacy. That is, many attributed the decline of the railroads to the belief by management that they were in the railroad business rather than the transportation business. Our mission statement begins, "The mission of Samford University is to nurture persons offering learning experiences and relationships within a Christian community." The mission statement does not say that we are in the university business or that we are a teaching organization. The mission frees us and encourages us to aim for the ends of learning without restricting us to the conventional academic means. Our mission puts us in the learning, not the university, business.

Now the question before us is, Are we creative and courageous enough to leave old paths and blaze new ones to become a community of learners and a community that learns? Pioneers and trailblazers usually do not come from those who are currently successful and highly respected. Those excelling in the current paradigms rarely break out of them. Nevertheless, aspiring academic institutions usually try to gain respect by copying and excelling in the conventions of the prestigious institutions. Our vision sets us on a different path: "Secure in its [Samford's] distinctive identity, choosing to be a developing model rather than replicating another, ..."

Nevertheless, it will not be easy for a southern institution with little name recognition that is identified with a large religious community to feel secure in breaking academic conventions. Our faculty and administrators understandably covet the approval of their regional and national counterparts as much as other academics do. We bounce back and forth on our definition of quality. In one situation, we cite conventional standards of academic quality, for example, rising scores of freshman classes, impressive experiences and credentials of new faculty, growing endowments, and a beautiful campus. However, when we talk about QI, we focus on customer satisfaction—students, parents, employers, and religious constituency. The first case deals with recognition; the second, with effectiveness. The recognition route reinforces staying with the current, dominant paradigms of the academy. We will begin to break paradigms when we completely commit to our mission and vision.

"What Impact Has TQM Had on the Leadership at Samford?"

As Senge (1990) makes clear, organizations learn as the mental models of the people in them change. These changes continue only when openness and merit are respected. By *openness,* Senge means that ideas and opinions are exposed in formal meetings with the leader, not afterward at coffee when he or she is not around. By *merit,* he means adopting the idea that is best for the institution, not the one that the leader likes.

We also struggle with implementing Deming's (1986) view that the quality leader seeks to remove obstacles that keep faculty and staff from taking pride in their work. He calls for substituting leadership for supervision. As a technician said to me in an informal moment, "Anybody can manage by making rules." He went on to explain that he knew what needed to be done in his technical area. He did not need more rules. He needed help, not necessarily more people, to accomplish his job.

On this point, our administrators, like those in most academic institutions and organizations, do not act arbitrarily or make rules capriciously. They seek wide input before they decide, but they still decide. We are not at the third stage suggested by DeMott (n.d., pp. 1–7), at which administrators say: "This is your decision to make. Here are the constraints and parameters. Let's move forward." Furthermore, we realize that many in the university, having been conditioned to an authoritarian approach, may not want the responsibility of deciding. It is not just that administrators hold the power to themselves but that other personnel assign all responsibility to them.

Our journey has just begun, and this chapter is as incomplete as the journey. For all our struggles, our president says that he would begin again, although wiser. So would I.

References

Barker, J. A. *Discovering the Future: The Business of Paradigms.* St. Paul, Minn.: ILI Press, 1989.

Deming, W. E. *Out of the Crisis.* Cambridge: Center for Advanced Engineering Study, Massachusetts Institute of Technology, 1986.

DeMott, J. *Team Training for Process Improvement: Training.* Philomath, Ore.: J. DeMott Company, n.d.

Kotler, P., and Fox, K.F.A. *Strategic Marketing for Educational Institutions.* Englewood Cliffs, N.J.: Prentice Hall, 1975.

Senge, P. M. *The Fifth Discipline: The Art and Practice of the Learning Organization.* New York: Doubleday, 1990.

JOHN W. HARRIS is assistant to the provost for quality assessment at Samford University, Birmingham, Alabama.

PART TWO

Continuous
Improvement Results

Quality management staff help academic departments to initiate quality improvement in response to self-study reports and external peer reviews.

Building on External Quality Assessment to Achieve Continuous Improvement

Hans A. Acherman, Liesbeth A.A.M. van Welie, Carla T. M. Laan

The Dutch Association of Universities initiated an external quality assessment program through peer reviews in 1987. This program is discipline oriented (all programs in a specific discipline are assessed by the same peer group) and cyclical (every program is assessed in a six-year cycle). Many aspects of the program utilize traditional peer review procedures, including the development of a departmental self-study and report. These procedures cause varying amounts of internal departmental debate and reflection. Nationally, the program elevated the level of discussion about educational issues, including concern for the improvement of educational quality.

Findings of the Peer Groups

As the number of completed reviews increases, the concerns and recommendations of the peer groups are becoming more explicit. In general, four improvement trends are emerging. First, many, mostly limited, adjustments in the structure and content of the curricula are being implemented by departments almost immediately after the site visit and peer group report is submitted. Second, more fundamental changes occur much later. These changes are developed in response to growing uneasiness about traditional approaches to education. Third, awareness that the educational process itself is at the heart of most problems is increasing. For example, students complain that unstructured curricula take too long to complete. Fourth, there is debate within the government on imposed boundary conditions, such as open admissions and limitations to four-year curricula. Peer review also established that change to the educational process can only be brought about from within the institutions themselves.

Change from Within

The interests, commitment, and activities of the individual teacher are the means by which we can improve learning and develop more effective curricula. As such, a periodic visit to a department by a peer review team is at best a useful incentive for educational improvement. Since the peer review reports do not address management skills or decision-making processes, most departments do not know how to respond to the reports or translate recommendations or criticisms into action.

At the University of Amsterdam, we initiated a project to help departments undertake a process of continuous improvement as a follow-up to the periodic external quality assessment self-studies and peer review reports. In 1991, the university's executive board appointed a quality project manager in the office of education and research. The manager has five responsibilities: to identify factors that influence the quality of education, to describe and facilitate quality improvement in a decentralized manner tailor-made to each department, to develop tools to measure educational effectiveness, to develop tools to measure improvement, and to identify the management skills needed to initiate innovation and change.

Since we are convinced that you must address educational improvement through the interaction between the professor and the student, our main task is to facilitate the dialogue about education among faculty. This requires us to discuss with faculty questions about the definition of quality in each specific situation, identifying successful teaching-learning approaches, and identifying how and where improvements can be made and who should be involved. The many requests from departments for assistance exceed even our expectations.

In choosing projects and project teams, we look for change agents— faculty, students, and administrators—who are committed to improvement and innovation. We also look for multidisciplinary or cross-functional teams to encourage participants to think more consciously about their personal contributions to the process and the impact of their activities on other customers.

Process Consultants

Departments often ask us for answers and solutions to their questions and problems. We explain that our role is to help the department find its own solutions to educational improvement, to facilitate a learning process that enables the department to manage its own development and strengthen its problem-solving capacity. We do so by participating in all steps of the review, by listening, by asking questions, and by engaging in dialogue. Our role is that of process consultants.

One aspect of our role is to help departments avoid quick fixes in favor of continuous improvement solutions. Faster is slower. Slower is better. There are no simple solutions for such problems as student motivation, the qualifications of instructors or students, or the process of self-evaluation. These and other problems are also highly interrelated, so that changes in one aspect of the issue are likely to produce changes in other aspects. Improvement is realized only after long-term, deliberate commitment to changes.

Department of Environmental Studies

A peer review committee visited environmental studies in 1989. The committee recommended finding a means for increasing cooperation and integration among the several divisions in the department. The executive board supported the committee report and advised the department on cooperating with the quality management team. The department council appointed a process improvement steering committee composed of students, faculty, a student counselor, the department council chair, the vice chair of the department's educational committee, and the vice dean who served as chair. We identified the vice dean and the student counselor as the most important and willing change agents. We worked with the committee to improve its listening skills, to use consensus to identify good initiatives for changes, to focus on individuals willing to implement improvements, and to provide appropriate motivation, support, and rewards.

Today's Problems, Yesterday's Solutions

Senge (1990) observes that the problems of today come from yesterday's solutions. Five years ago, the university created the divisions in the department of environmental studies with no particular attempt to promote or instill unity among them. Accordingly, we did not know what kind of cooperation to expect in studying educational quality within the department as a whole.

Nonetheless, the steering committee organized discussions with faculty and students from all divisions on the topic of educational quality. Both faculty and student involvement are necessary because they are the ones most likely to know how to improve the educational process. Without such involvement, it is unlikely that faculty and students will commit to the solutions for improvement.

The steering committee began its dialogue around the self-studies of the several divisions. These self-studies contained many ideas and plans for improving quality, but they lacked specifics. By beginning with material generated by the divisions, the steering committee demonstrated respect for the ideas and efforts of the divisions. Many faculty recognized the improved atmosphere and expressed pleasure that someone was asking, listening, and paying attention. The vice dean, now dean, for environmental studies also used the activities of the steering committee to learn more about the divisions in the department and developed a vision for environmental studies from the bottom up.

Results

Several projects are now under way in the department as a result of the steering committee's deliberations: improvements in the information about environmental studies provided to students, prospective students, and high school teachers; improvements in student guidance programs; and introduction of a curriculum oriented toward problem solving. In choosing projects, we apply three important principles: First, start somewhere in the organization that is likely to become an effective point for change and where visible results are most likely. Second, do not start with too many ambitions or with extremely sensitive problems. Third, do not start with projects that are so small that the activities and the results will be invisible.

To facilitate the effort, project leaders for each proposal are taking courses in project management. In addition, the student counselor on the steering committee is now head of a bureau of educational policy in the department. Her responsibilities include guiding and coordinating the projects.

Other initiatives under way in the department include appointing a new recruitment official, new courses in several majors, a new program in geographical information systems, a new course in career planning, a new student evaluation process, and organization of an alumni group.

Guiding Principles

Several important principles are guiding the continuous quality improvement effort at the University of Amsterdam: The change strategy for each department must be tailor-made—there is no recipe for change. Managing quality is not a top-down activity, but external pressure can hasten the initiation of the effort. Trust people and their abilities, and assume that they wish to do good work; no one is to blame for problems. One cannot push improvement; there is no place for quick fixes. Faculty involvement is critical; they are the experts and the individuals most able to initiate change in the educational milieu. Commitment from management is critical to the overall attainment of quality improvement. Quality management requires a paradigm shift. Such a shift becomes possible when the principles of quality management are clearly presented, discussed, and understood.

Changing the culture begins with trust. When mutual respect is achieved, a major step toward quality improvement is realized.

Reference

Senge, P. M. *The Fifth Discipline: The Art and Practice of the Learning Organization.* New York: Doubleday, 1990.

HANS A. ACHERMAN *is deputy secretary general at the University of Amsterdam and a former project manager of quality at the Verenigde Samenwerkende Nederlandse Universiteiten (Association of Universities in The Netherlands).*

LIESBETH A.A.M. VAN WELIE *is quality manager of education at the University of Amsterdam and a former secondary school principal.*

CARLA T. M. LAAN *is associate quality manager at the University of Amsterdam.*

Total Quality Management represents a set of ideas that we are happy to discuss in the classroom but less willing to practice. Personal experiences demonstrate how these concepts can improve an instructor's performance.

Total Quality Management in the Classroom: A Personal Odyssey

J. Keith Ord

The introductory statistics class for the M.B.A. program is known at many business schools as a dog. Often, the only unresolved question is whether the students or the faculty like it less. In fall 1990, when my number came up for that assignment in the Smeal College of Business Administration at The Pennsylvania State University, I undertook the task with considerable reluctance. The course proceeded down the dogged path that I and others had plotted in the past. Eventually, both the students and I battled our way to the end of the semester. I knew that the journey had not gone particularly well, and this impression was duly confirmed by the teaching evaluations and accompanying comments.

For recreation, I run regularly, and I compete in a number of races each year. In the thirty years that I have been running, I only once dropped out of a race. That was more than twenty-five years ago, and the memory still haunts me. I am not by nature a quitter, and so I decided to look at the issues surrounding the introductory statistics course to explore how it might be improved.

In 1986, several statisticians from leading business schools and industry started an annual conference now known as MSMESB (Making Statistics More Effective in Schools of Business). At these meetings, there are usually three tracks: one on teaching statistics, one on quality issues, and one on statistical research issues in a functional area of business. Typically, 100 to 150 people whose responsibilities include the teaching of statistics attend these meetings. I started attending these meetings in 1989, but I focused on the content issues rather than on the pedagogy. The time had come to think not only about preaching Total Quality Management (TQM) but also about practicing TQM.

Because I had always recoiled from the wild-eyed prophets who seize upon TQM or any other fashionable cure for the world's ills, I moved forward cautiously at first. To my surprise, I became more excited as the venture proceeded and I found myself actually enjoying the M.B.A. classes. In retrospect, while the methods that I adopted required somewhat greater effort of me, they are well known and could be adopted readily by any instructor in statistics or other subjects.

The first step was to increase the discussion of quality control methods in the course. I introduced the testing of hypotheses in the context of control methods and reinforced the message with a rather lame imitation of W. Edwards Deming's presentation of the red-bead game. It was well received by the class. Although this activity is specific to statistics, the main innovation introduced minute reports at the end of each class. Students respond to the same three questions each time: What was the main message of today's class? What did you learn? What did you not understand?

The students' responses are analyzed between classes and used as input to the next class. The first two questions are intended to encourage a personal review of the day's proceedings, and they are valuable for general monitoring. The third question serves as a very useful check on potential problems. A Pareto chart analysis of the responses highlights the principal difficulties, and I review them at the next class.

Initially, I tended to review everything that students mentioned. The result was that my overreviewing soon placed well up on the Pareto chart! Subsequently, the 20 percent of problems that arise 80 percent of the time are dealt with in class, and the remainder are discussed after class or during office hours. When I forget to take the "official" minute report forms to class and ask students to write their ideas on a blank sheet of paper, the response rate drops markedly.

A more substantial midsemester review produced several useful suggestions. The most notable is the introduction of statistical issues. The students refer to this process as "show and tell." During each class, a team summarizes a statistical study gleaned from a recent newspaper or magazine, and we discuss the strengths and weaknesses of the approach used. Sources vary from the Wall Street Journal to U.S.A. Today and Parade magazine. The topics are diverse, and some useful insights usually emerge.

Although I felt much better about the course by the end of the semester, that is an imperfect measure of success. More direct measures are provided by the end-of-semester evaluation instruments used for all courses. The two principal questions relate to the overall quality of the course (QC) and the overall quality of the instructor (QI). We score the questions on a seven-point scale running from 1 (poor) through 3 (average) and 4 (good) up to 7 (outstanding). Evaluations from two groups of forty students in each year showed that QC and QI scores both improved. The results can be summarized as follows:

	1990	1991
Quality of course	4.19	5.18
Quality of instructor	4.42	5.78

The fall 1992 student evaluation scores were 5.08 for QC and 5.76 for QI, sustaining the gains achieved between 1990 and 1991.

Students are assigned to sections by the M.B.A. office to achieve a balance of ability and experience across sections. Hence, there is no reason to suspect any selection bias in class membership. Less formally, a number of students still stop by to ask statistical questions. Perhaps they want to get rich quick by analyzing stock market trends, but at least they want to try it in a statistically sound manner. (There have been no great successes that I know of, but perhaps they would not tell me.)

As should be true of any TQM project, I received a number of constructive suggestions for course improvements the next time around. A number of these ideas will impact the major restructuring of our M.B.A. program that is being implemented. For example, students expressed concern about being in different teams for each course, which made coordination difficult and led to uneven work loads. This year, we are using the same teams across a number of courses, which also serves to make the team interactions more sustained and realistic. Several suggestions on the presentation and ordering of course material will be incorporated, and some of the projects will be modified.

None of these innovations is earth-shattering, but they were not intended to be. However, by listening to our customers, we may gradually achieve improvement.

J. KEITH ORD is David McKinley Professor of Business Administration and professor of statistics at The Pennsylvania State University, University Park.

The plan-do-check-act cycle is used to design and evaluate course improvement experiments.

Improvements in Introductory Physics Courses

P. E. Sokol

A major problem identified in our large introductory physics classes at The Pennsylvania State University is that students spend too little time studying outside of class. Surveys of students in these courses suggest that they spend less than an hour outside of class for every hour in class. This is far less than the standard of two to three hours outside of class for every hour in class.

To address this problem, we made several modifications in our introductory quantum mechanics course. These changes were aimed at increasing the amount of time students spend studying outside of class. With an enrollment of 150, the course is large enough for a realistic test while small enough that new methods are easy to implement. Through the plan-do-check-act cycle, Total Quality Management (TQM) provides us with a tool that we can use to evaluate the effectiveness of these changes.

The plan for the changes is based on two assumptions: First, more study time improves performance. Second, there are many demands on student time. Thus, any changes to encourage students to spend more time outside the classroom must reward them for extra effort.

One of the most direct ways of increasing the time spent studying is to assign challenging homework problems, collect them, grade them, and give them substantial weight in the overall course grade. This is not a standard practice in our large introductory courses due to the large number of students who enroll.

The effort required to grade homework is quite substantial. To minimize the effort, we did not fully grade every homework problem but chose two problems at random for detailed grading, including constructive criticism.

To reward students for the extra effort, we counted homework for 50 percent of the course grade. We also abandoned grading on a curve and instituted an absolute grading scheme to discourage the collective laziness phenomenon. During recitation sections, we asked students to put homework problems on the board to foster peer recognition and encouragement.

To evaluate the effectiveness of these changes, we conducted a midsemester evaluation that included informal surveys. The results of one survey showed students spending nine hours of study time per week outside of class (Figure 6.1). Time spent on homework is also directly correlated to exam scores (Figure 6.2). While there is considerable scatter in the data, the results clearly show a correlation between homework and exam grades.

How did the customer—in this case, the students—view this heavy emphasis on homework? Figure 6.3 shows the results of a survey of the students' impressions of grading homework and using it as a large part of the final grade. More than 60 percent of the students thought it was a great idea and liked the deemphasis on make-or-break exams. However, almost 40 percent of the students did not like the new system. One student stated, "This is terrible! It's like having a take-home exam every week. I would prefer to just cram for exams and forget about it the rest of the time." This comment clearly illustrates how grading homework assignments accomplished the desired goals.

However, the students did not like the changes in the recitation format (Figure 6.4). Student interviews indicated that spending additional time

Figure 6.1. Student Study Time

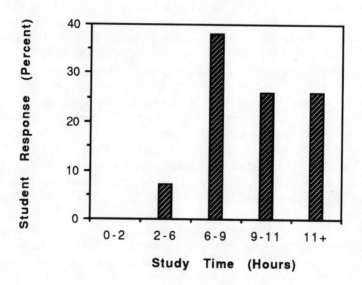

Figure 6.2. Homework-Exam Correlation

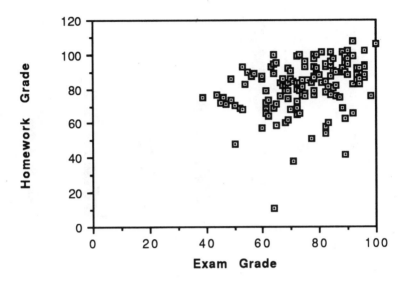

Figure 6.3. Homework Preference

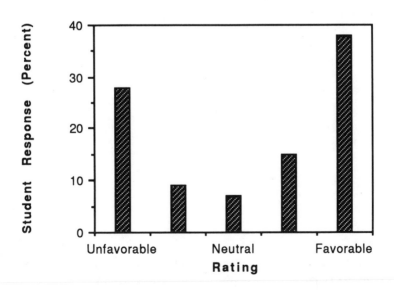

Figure 6.4. Recitation Format Preference

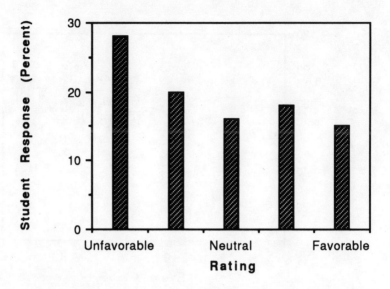

reviewing problems that were already completed, rather than covering new material, was not a particularly valuable way of spending recitation time.

Applying the plan-do-check-act cycle facilitated development and evaluation of instructional changes and guides future improvement efforts. Future tests will be aimed at determining the optimum balance between the extra effort needed to grade homework and increasing student activities outside of class.

P. E. SOKOL is associate professor of physics at The Pennsylvania State University, University Park.

Quality improvement principles and processes transform and revitalize an ailing nursing program through a systematic evaluation of teaching, advising, and admissions processes.

Bringing a Nursing Program Back to Life

Marian K. Baur

After eighteen months as dean of the Ida V. Moffett School of Nursing at Samford University, I was distressed to note a sudden and unexpected, dramatic drop in our graduates' success rate on the nationally standardized licensing examination for registered nurses (NCLEX-RN). The examination had been revised to focus on analytical reasoning ability. New test questions evolved from a recent national work setting analysis that attracted responses from approximately twenty thousand new graduate employees. The national council developed and implemented this altered testing format in July 1988 to better reflect the changed role and responsibility of newly employed graduates.

Our May 1988 A.S.N. degree graduates experienced some difficulty on the July 1988 examination. The success rate dropped to 80 percent from the 90 percent or higher rate that the school had enjoyed before the examination was revised. Other schools noted a similar downward trend in their graduates' success rate. At the peak of the nursing shortage, this national problem became the focus of serious discussion between nursing educators and employers of new graduates from all types of nursing programs.

As a new dean, I sensed that the school had some problems, but at this point I had not isolated specific issues that could have contributed to this decline in our success rate.

Before we award students the A.S.N. degree, we require them to take a two-semester-hour seminar that focuses on nursing history, trends, and issues faced in the practice setting. I taught this course in the fall 1988 term and found that students were totally dependent on me to lecture. Many students were not able or prepared to discuss assigned readings from the text, and they seemed unable, unwilling, or both to make inferences or use deductive methods. The students' attitude and lack of decision-making ability greatly concerned me. Further, their results on the February 1989 NCLEX-RN surprised and dismayed us when the success rate dropped to 45 percent.

We called two special faculty meetings and began our soul-searching and discussion. We started by looking at curriculum, faculty teaching strategies, student profiles, admissions criteria, organization, and clinical experiences. Rather than placing blame, we focused on system issues. Some of us left these lengthy meetings concerned and depressed because no one seemed willing to accept responsibility as teachers to identify and address the instructional issues that contributed to the students' lack of success. Instead, the group only identified some curricular issues and problems related to transfer students.

In fall 1989, the assistant to the provost for quality assessment and two nurse educators, serving as consultants, became vital and positive forces for change and self-examination as well as process evaluation. They approached their individual consultation opportunities in a collegial, supportive manner that encouraged and facilitated faculty-student input without attempting to attach blame to any one individual, group, or process. During this period, it became evident that a schism existed within the faculty of the school. Several faculty members involved students in discussion about problems in a manner that enhanced their expertise as educators in the eyes of the students while undermining the students' confidence in the abilities of the other teachers. They also openly stated to their faculty colleagues and in the nursing community at large that they had effected the resignation of one dean and they planned to do so again. These disruptive behaviors affected morale, enrollment, and credibility.

By spring 1990, several faculty resignations seemed to revitalize the remaining faculty members. Under the leadership of School of Nursing committee chairpersons, the self-study reports for impending professional reaccreditation began to evolve. We reviewed syllabi and brought curriculum changes to faculty for vigorous and open discussion and vote. We scrutinized existing admission criteria as well as the admission process itself. We committed to focus on service to the prospective, qualified student. We determined not to be driven by our concern for numbers, and we received full support from our administration.

A change in staffing and a revised job description refocused recruitment, enrollment, and initial advisement responsibilities. Faculty members again assumed responsibility for ongoing academic advisement. A newly created position of assistant to the dean for enrollment management began recruiting with key colleagues in universities and hospitals and interviewing all prospective students. School of Nursing staff members joined the recruitment team and began completing information cards for the university admissions office. We all realized that we needed to represent our school and university to our primary customer—the student and his or her family.

The success rate for the NCLEX-RN steadily increased: July 1989, 69 percent; February 1990, 91 percent; July 1990, 89 percent; and February 1991, 100 percent. The rate continues to hover between 90 percent and 100 percent. All students now state during their exit interviews that they would recommend the school, and the admission forms that we receive now often list Samford graduates as friends. Enrollment doubled, attrition declined, and a new energy pervades the school. Accreditation reviews proceeded in an almost flawless manner, and both the A.S.N. and B.S.N. programs received full continuing accreditation.

Faculty, staff, and student involvement and a commitment to the quality assessment process are responsible for this transformation. To sustain it, we continue to encourage and provide faculty and staff with opportunities for professional regeneration.

MARIAN K. BAUR is dean of the Ida V. Moffett School of Nursing at Samford University, Birmingham, Alabama.

A focus on customer needs and organizational processes led to a complete reorganization and redefinition of all library service positions.

Revitalization of Library Service

Jean Thomason

What do you do with a library organization that is twenty-five years old, overstaffed in one department and understaffed in another, and that has procedures developed around personalities and a demoralized library staff? Using quality methods and tools, we reorganized the Samford University library.

The professional librarians assumed the responsibility for the reorganization task and became the quality team. Suggestions for the new organization could be submitted as written comments or in chart form. We encouraged individuals to design an organization as if none currently existed and to submit as many plans as they desired. The librarians composing the reorganization team identified four objectives: Improve service to the customer, reduce duplication of processes, define processes better, and empower the library staff.

Because some members of the team had worked together for years, we developed guidelines for group behavior to overcome prejudices and standard responses. We displayed these guidelines at every meeting: Support all information with facts. Base decisions on logic, not emotion. Strive to reach a consensus. If consensus is not reached, the director will make the decision.

We held several brainstorming sessions to evaluate library operations. We asked, What is involved in this operation? Where can this operation best be performed? Which other operations does this one relate to? After evaluating the operations, the team studied the plans recommended by staff and chose six for careful consideration. For each plan, we evaluated its service goals, operations, and work processes. The team considered moving operations and departments, dispensing entirely with departments, and the appropriate number of departments. We attempted to visualize every reasonable structure. This type of examination emphasized the service and work philosophy created by the plans proposed. After this concentrated study, the team narrowed the list to two plans.

A detailed discussion ensued to gain an understanding of every aspect of the two plans and anticipate each process that they entailed. We used an affinity diagram to determine any unresolved questions. After answering these questions, the team selected a circular organizational chart that places the director at the center and individual units around the circumference. The circle conveys the equality among units. Each unit is empowered to perform its function, yet they are also committed to working together. Each unit has a coordinator whose role is to serve as its facilitator.

After choosing the organizational structure, the team investigated the number of staff needed. The ideal number emerged as eleven librarians and twenty and one-half support staff. Since these numbers exceeded the current ones, we returned to the drawing board. Team members conferred again with staff members to define tasks further. We used this information to reduce the number of needed staff to ten librarians and eighteen support staff—numbers that stayed within the current budget. We wrote job descriptions for each position in the new organization.

To find the right position for each staff member, the team declared all positions except library director vacant. Each person requested three positions in order of preference. Overlaps in choice were resolved by the director. This process worked well. Every librarian received his or her first choice, except one who received her second. This individual not only accepted the second choice but also displayed creativity and innovation in the position and became a genuine asset to the organization.

After the professional librarians were placed in their new positions, the support staff bid on positions. Two people did not receive their first choice. We resolved one position to the person's satisfaction. The other individual resigned.

The reevaluation process took seven months. Two-thirds of the staff, including nine of the ten professional librarians and ten of the nineteen support staff, are in new or revised positions.

The tangible results of the reorganization can be reviewed under three headings: increased service, improved service, and improved processes. To increase service, we increased the staffing of the reference desk by 21 percent, and nonstudent staffing of the circulation desk by 64 percent. To improve service, we separated the reference and circulation units and combined the interlibrary loan and resource retrieval services. We improved processes in a number of ways: All order processes are now handled in a single area. We created an office manager position and established a work area for the processing of manuscripts in the special collection. We reduced professional staff by one and increased support staff by three. Finally, we established a new position of associate director.

Other improvements are not as easy to list, but they are also very significant. The library is becoming service oriented, and we are learning to think about our customers. We are also discovering that the control we desired for years is within our reach. Evaluating processes rather than seeking quick fixes is still a struggle, but we are learning from our successes.

JEAN THOMASON is associate director of the library at Samford University, Birmingham, Alabama.

At the University of Pennsylvania, potential savings are one criterion
for selecting pilot projects in Total Quality Management.

Realizing Financial Savings Through Total Quality Management

Karen Archambault Miselis

In fall 1990, the quality council appointed by the executive vice president for finance and administration at the University of Pennsylvania adopted a set of criteria for identifying projects to test the quality improvement process. These criteria included the likelihood of success, manageable size, campuswide visibility and impact, a focus on cross-functional processes, and potential for savings through the elimination of scrap, rework, and unnecessary complexity. With respect to the prospect of saving resources, the executive vice president in particular believed that acceptance of total quality principles both within the area of finance and administration and across the university as a whole could be achieved more quickly and openly if people realized that Total Quality Management (TQM) could actually free up resources.

Ensuring Timely Recovery of Sponsored Research Funding

The quality council appointed an eight-member finance quality improvement team to examine the failure to receive timely payments from external sponsors of research projects. This failure had resulted in financial losses to the university. Reports collected from the central accounting system indicated that the problem contributed to an unfunded balance of approximately $18.9 million. The finance quality improvement team identified three types of costs resulting from this unfunded balance: the cost of funds relating to unfunded balances, lost funds due to uncollectible accounts, and the loss of goodwill and jeopardized future funding. The team's goal was to reduce all three costs.

After clarifying the problem, the team began by flowcharting the process of establishing and managing research accounts. In so doing, the team discovered a number of areas in which errors could occur. The team reviewed all research accounts that had negative cash balances to quantify the size and impact of the problem. Through brainstorming, the team identified possible causes of errors and then used a detailed study of accounts with negative cash balances to examine the proposed causes.

After reviewing processes and analyzing data, the team outlined four primary areas of responsibility within the process: the schools, the Office of Research Administration (ORA), research accounting (RA), and sponsors. They theorized that many symptoms resulted from communication breakdowns between these areas of responsibility. The lack of university guidelines for negotiating ideal or even minimum payment terms appeared as the root cause in the breakdown of communication between ORA and research sponsors. The team defined optimal payment terms and minimum monthly reimbursement of costs. ORA issued a policy memo for sponsors defining optimal payment terms and minimum standards. This memo is yielding successful results. We remedied the two root causes to the communication breakdown between ORA and RA by revising the set of codes to be used by both offices and by creating a new form, the account information sheet, to transmit the required information from ORA to RA. The invoice serves as a communications vehicle between RA and sponsor. Through voice of the customer sessions with sponsors, the team got suggestions resulting in the development and implementation of a more effective invoice.

To hold on to gains already realized, the team proposed quarterly reports through 1992 on the aggregated net cash balance on all sponsored programs, the total cash balance for overdrafted accounts, an aging analysis of receivables, and the number and total amount of lock box receipts by month. Several new teams developed from this initial team when it became clear that the management of sponsored research accounts is an extremely complicated process that has many opportunities for improvement.

Both team members and others reacted favorably to the project. The team believed that the TQM structure, methodology, and tools made it easier to identify the source of the problems. Because the team included cross-functional representatives with a shared desire to solve a problem and not place blame, we made progress in recognizing problems and working to solve them. The focus that TQM places on planning and continuous improvement taught team members that their improvements, even if small, serve as important stepping stones leading to future process improvements. Team members also learned that TQM projects involve a considerable time commitment and that the teams need to communicate constantly with the managers of responsible areas as well as with the quality council to reduce fear and resistance to change.

Reducing the Number of Research Account Overdrafts

The second project focused on overdrafted research accounts in the amount of $13 million. Since this problem involved the schools—primarily medicine, arts and sciences, and engineering and applied science—rather than the central administration, the project team membership was drawn entirely from the schools.

However, the first session made it clear that the team needed to recruit members from either ORA or RA. The team needed their particular expertise and their commitment in considering possible causes of the problem. The quality council chose to assign one new member from RA to the team.

The team brainstormed the possible causes of the problem and found that a large percentage of budget overdrafts—perhaps 95 percent—cleared up over time. Their review suggested that the sponsored account budgeting process is complicated, ill-defined, and burdensome and that a large number of budget overdrafts are temporary and not actual expenditures in excess of award amount. The team found several causes of the overdraft problem and recommended a multiple solution to address them.

However, the team encountered difficulties in both the investigative process and in its attempts to implement solutions. As a result, the team's experiences indicate areas for caution in the formation of quality improvement teams. For example, those in charge of the offices with the authority to change the process under study must fully support the team, and the team membership should include sufficient members from the offices in charge of the process. In the case of the research account overdrafts project, the team encountered difficulties in acquiring necessary information since most of the team members were not from the central offices responsible for the management of research accounts but rather were school or departmental financial officers. Similarly, many of the solutions recommended by the team required implementation by central offices. Because of the limited membership on the team from the responsible offices, it was more difficult to gain agreement for the implementation of the solutions. Finally, the delays frustrated the team members, especially those from customer departments, who worked on the project over and above their regular responsibilities.

KAREN ARCHAMBAULT MISELIS is executive vice president for finance and administration at the Franklin Institute, Philadelphia, and former associate dean for administration in the School of Arts and Sciences at the University of Pennsylvania.

A quality improvement culture evolves when team practices are carried into the everyday office environment.

Teamwork Improves Office Climate

Susan K. Winck

The Smeal College of Business Administration at The Pennsylvania State University selected the advising center as the pilot unit for a continuous quality improvement project. No one in the center had any previous training or knowledge of continuous quality improvement. Advising center staff selected two processes for improvement: new student orientation and student intake and reception. In addition to the process improvement results, we realized an important side benefit: a positive change in attitude among staff, supervisors, and students.

Promoting Cooperation

Team ground rules promoted a cooperative approach that carried over from team activities to subsequent staff meetings. Staff members more readily exhibit a desire to listen to one another's ideas and then work together to develop a consensus for a particular decision or procedure.

Consensus. Decision by consensus means that everyone agrees to support the group decision even if one does not agree with the decision. Consensus building takes time, involves all team members in discussion, ensures that concerns are stated and understood by all members of the team, and sometimes involves the listing of pros and cons before the decision is made. It can be applied to any decision-making process that brings together a group of individuals who have many different ideas and experiences with a particular process.

Avoiding Blame. The focus on process also moves individuals away from pointing fingers or blame. Instead, conversations develop around such process evaluation issues as these: What can we do to correct this process?

NEW DIRECTIONS FOR INSTITUTIONAL RESEARCH, no. 78, Summer 1993 © Jossey-Bass Publishers

What steps did we miss? How can we prevent this error from occurring next time?

We, rather than *they* or *them,* is heard more often. Every staff member has greater ownership and responsibility for what is happening. Staff members see their ideas for change implemented and as a result are ready to accept responsibility for successful change.

Focus on Students as Customers. Identifying students as our primary customers gave the treatment of students new importance. Students are no longer viewed as an interruption but as the reason for our existence.

We learned that our preconceived ideas about students are not always correct. We learned the value of using data rather than intuition to determine program emphases.

Conclusion

The goal of Total Quality Management is not how many process improvement teams can be created but how to create an environment for improvement. A team approach to complex tasks is time-consuming, but it can create a better sense of community in which tasks can be accomplished more effectively and efficiently.

SUSAN K. WINCK *is administrative director of undergraduate programs in the Smeal College of Business Administration at The Pennsylvania State University, University Park.*

Perseverance pays off with measurable improvements.

Total Quality Management Is *Total* at Fox Valley Technical College

Carol R. Tyler

In 1986, Fox Valley Technical College (FVTC) began applying Total Quality Management (TQM) principles and tools to its management, service, and instructional processes. Over the last six years, FVTC examined and improved numerous processes. These improvements resulted in more satisfied customers, and often they reduced costs. While such outcomes demonstrate the dividends paid by TQM, there are often additional implications. This chapter demonstrates both these positive outcomes and the other effects in brief discussions of nine process improvement projects.

Reducing Cycle Time for the Processing of Student Applications

At FVTC, student applications for admission are sent to the admissions office, which processes them and then sends them to the appropriate instructional division counselor. At various times, an eager student reached the division counselor ahead of the application. To better serve students, the dean of student services and the two support staff personnel who process the applications agreed to apply various TQM tools to reduce the five to seven days it was taking to get the application into the counselor's hands. Through brainstorming and the collection of data, they reduced the cycle time to twenty-four hours and maintained that gain for more than two years.

As a result, students are better served and counselors can now access student records more readily to discuss students' application status with them. This positive outcome is tempered by the fact that it takes additional part-time people to process the applications. However, the staff who process the applications developed and implemented a plan of staggered work schedules so as to also cover the main switchboard and information desk from 7:00 A.M. to 8:00 P.M.

Decreasing Employee Accidents and Worker Compensation Claims

As part of a process management course offered to managers at FVTC, the vice-president of human resources looked into employee accidents and related costs. Using Pareto charts, he identified the accidents that were the most costly, the departments in which they occurred, the type of accidents that occurred, and the frequency with which they occurred.

These steps reduced worker compensation premiums by $51,000 and improved the college's preventive proactive safety program. We have developed more and better safety in-services for staff and students, and employees are coming up with more ideas related to safety. Our worker compensation carrier is charting and graphing safety information for us on a quarterly basis.

Assessing the Customer Focus at FVTC

FVTC offered training in quality awareness to every staff member over a three-year period. A major thrust of the training was to instill a customer focus. We were not sure how to assess whether the customer focus had increased until the institutional researcher noted an increasing number of requests for her services. Through collection of data, she observed the following changes: The requests for research services doubled. The requests from individuals went down and requests from departments and problem-solving teams went up. Finally, requests for research design experienced similar increases.

In short, increasing numbers of FVTC staff members are doing customer research, and more of the research is being designed, administered, and put to immediate use by teams.

Some processes definitely changed for the better as teams invested in the research. Many teams had positive first experiences using focus groups or surveys. At the same time, the work load of the research office increased dramatically. It became more challenging to deliver quality and timely research services and more difficult to set priorities faced with the increase in requests for ad hoc surveys from teams.

Merging Quality and Policy Structures

In initiating its TQM process, FVTC created many new committees, including a quality improvement council. That council had fourteen members composed of representatives of various employee classifications in the organization. A twenty-two-member administrative council also existed. FVTC charged the quality improvement council with planning and monitoring the quality initiative and the administrative council with making policy. After five years, we merged the two councils for both symbolic and practical reasons. We used a carefully designed process with maximum staff input for this process. A new ten-member council is charged with both policy and quality. The president is a permanent member, and the elected members include three faculty members, three support staff, and three managers. The new total quality leadership team flowcharted its processes and practices for consensus decision making.

The new team began with systems and processes in place and well understood. The added perspective of faculty and support staff continues to be valuable. However, almost twenty managers lost their seats on the policy-making council. Not surprisingly, some of them feel disenfranchised.

Revising Management Performance Appraisal Criteria

In checking the status of a quality-related project with a manager, the quality coordinator heard, "Look, you're a nice guy, and you have a worthwhile project, but I don't report to you, you don't pay my salary, and you don't evaluate me, so your project goes to the bottom of my pile." The link between regular assignments and quality initiatives was not seamless. We did not want to abandon individual performance appraisal, but we recognized that we needed to do something. That year, we rewrote some of the criteria affecting management merit increases to support quality improvement practices. The next year, we strengthened that language. The areas include the use of FVTC customer-oriented "standards" as a basis for improvement, the use of process management to improve processes, the use of team-building concepts, and the use of customer service techniques.

This step resulted in increased activity in these areas and better documentation. The managers and vice president of one administrative division received their individual merit increases, threw them into a single pot, took some off the top for a staff party, then split the pot evenly. As a result of these measures, our understanding of what other departments do has increased, and we are realizing the importance of the effect of what we do on the total picture. Ideas are increasingly shared, and the unity strengthened among managers. Employees feel more appreciated, and they are integrating quality into their daily activities. These positive outcomes are offset by the negative feelings that some units displayed toward those units showing initiative.

Creating a User-Friendly Student Services Location

The dean of student services used student input to design a new student services area that brought all functions to a common location. Focus groups yielded some wonderful insights, among them being that returning adult students are fearful of opening a door and walking into an office. As a result, the entire open student services area is designed with counters that are easy to approach. Students also designed an ongoing service evaluation process. Called "Give Us a Grade," this process uses point-of-service evaluations at all areas of student services.

The open environment provides a one-stop service-oriented atmosphere. Direct, timely feedback from our customers provides student services staff with continuous opportunities to improve our processes. Although customers sometimes feel saturated with customer service surveys, most students still appreciate the opportunity to evaluate the service and provide direct feedback regarding the student services division.

Creating a Self-Managing Class

In 1990, FVTC introduced a two-year associate degree program for quality improvement process specialists. We used quality principles and strategies to design the program and deliver the courses. The program developer took this one step further by creating a self-managing class. Specific strategies include the removal of the traditional grading structure to be more consistent with Deming's philosophy regarding performance appraisals; collaborative learning projects; teach-to-learn and learn-to-teach projects; and classroom time for long-term course projects.

Students often spend extra time outside of class on group activities. The class is developing more active learners, creating a relaxed environment, and promoting teamwork. These benefits are offset by the fact that the need to replace the traditional grading structure requires us to develop an outcome-based language to define performance objectives. We also require alternate assessment tools.

Making Program Graduates Competent in Quality

After practicing continuous improvement strategies for several years, we saw that although students benefited from the improvement of processes and services, many graduated from FVTC with no formal knowledge of TQM. This seemed both an irony and an injustice in a college whose mission is education for employment. The vice president of academic affairs created a quality competencies task force that identified core competency areas in TQM and developed a plan to integrate these competencies into general studies courses and into every occupational and technical program. The plan is to guarantee TQM competence in all program graduates.

A knowledge of TQM is a decided advantage for students in securing employment. This fact has renewed faculty interest in TQM. By the same token, TQM is now one of many other across-the-curriculum initiatives, including minority and gender issues and ethics. Courses become increasingly crowded, and some teachers become frustrated.

Simplifying Operational Planning

The planning office at FVTC realized that its process might be serving its own needs better than those of its customers. To improve the planning process, the planning office surveyed participants regarding their level of satisfaction. Customers replied: Give us information earlier, give us feedback throughout the process rather than at the end, and simplify the forms. The planning office simplified the forms. It releases information earlier, and it continues to monitor customer satisfaction.

Planning office staff appreciate being asked, and they are benefiting from implemented improvements. Nevertheless, the multiple stages of the planning cycle make it difficult to address immediately every area needing improvement.

CAROL R. TYLER is an instructor at Fox Valley Technical College, Appleton, Wisconsin.

PART THREE

Methods, Tools, and Techniques

Through Hoshin planning, individual units discover that they can integrate planning and Total Quality Management into their daily work.

Hoshin Planning Applies Total Quality Management to the Planning Process

Mary Ann Heverly, Jerome S. Parker

Hoshin, or breakthrough, planning is the Total Quality Management (TQM) method of integrating strategic planning into the daily work of all units in an organization. By targeting an organization's critical processes, Hoshin planning generates breakthroughs that help to achieve the organization's strategic goals, and it internally aligns the daily work of individual units with the organizational vision and strategic plan. Delaware County Community College (DCCC) adapted the Hoshin planning model outlined by King (1989) and GOAL/QPC (GOAL/QPC Research Committee, 1989). Figure 12.1, a matrix flowchart outlining the Hoshin planning process steps and the people involved at different steps in the process, shows how we adapted the Hoshin model.

Hoshin Planning and the TQM Paradigm

Five characteristics of Hoshin planning derive from the TQM paradigm: specificity and focus, continuous improvement, daily management and data, total staff involvement, and continuous communication. This section reviews these characteristics and describes how we implemented them at DCCC. (Other institutions represented in this volume that used Hoshin planning to identify critical processes are the University of Pennsylvania and Oregon State University; see Miselis, this volume; Howard, this volume.)

Specificity and Focus. All TQM methods and tools have the ultimate goal of focusing improvement efforts into high-leverage activities, that is, activities that conserve resources while maximizing quality improvement. Hoshin planning is no exception; its goal is to identify a small number of

 67

Figure 12.1. DCCC's Strategic Planning Process

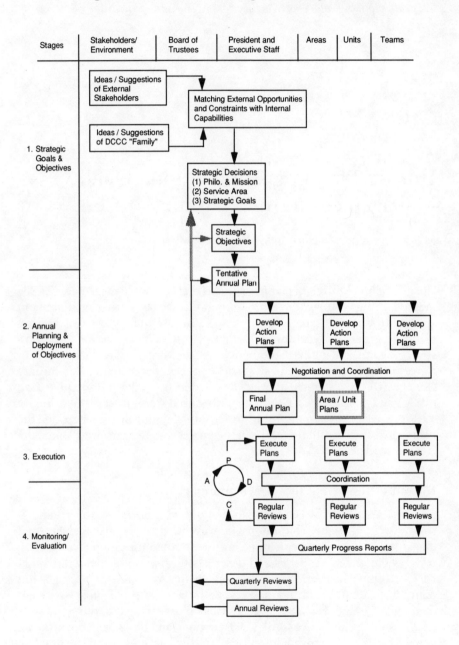

strategic areas as the organization's primary targets for breakthrough objectives. In traditional planning, an organization can identify a small set of areas to target, but these areas tend to proliferate when they are translated into specific objectives. Such proliferation can overwhelm staff and lessen their commitment to the planning process.

The contrast between the two approaches becomes clear if we compare DCCC's strategic plan for the 1980s, which was developed with traditional methods, with its Hoshin plan developed for the 1990s. Although both plans identified a small number of strategic areas (four in the plan for the 1980s, three in the plan for the 1990s), the plan for the 1980s was translated into sixty-six objectives, whereas the plan for the 1990s had only twenty-three objectives.

Continuous Improvement. The Hoshin planning process itself is subjected to continuous improvement, based on the institution's capabilities and on changes in the internal and external environment. This feature makes Hoshin planning a responsive and flexible method that can adapt quickly to changing demands.

At DCCC, the plan for the 1980s was reviewed annually to assess the results of each year's plan. However, many events in the course of a year could affect the priority of some objectives and the capability of the college to achieve others. The use of Hoshin planning for the 1990s is forcing regular examination of the planning process as it unfolds. Quarterly reviews serve as a reality check on the plans developed at the beginning of the annual planning cycle. The purpose of the reviews is to identify problems upstream that can serve as opportunities to support continuous improvement of unit plans and their implementation. Such improvement reduces the anxiety and guilt that the annual review of progress often provokes, and it eliminates strategic objectives that changed conditions and capabilities have made unattainable. Another positive result is the integration of planning with daily work. In the past, we tended to focus on strategic objectives only at the beginning of the cycle and then to shelve them until the annual review.

Daily Management and Data. The success of Hoshin planning depends on effective practice of daily management: identifying a unit's key processes, charting them, identifying data elements that can be used to measure process steps and process outputs, and carrying out a plan for gathering these data. The resulting monitoring systems identify areas for improvement and provide baseline measures for the plans and targets that we develop. Taken together, these systems provide information regarding the capability of the organization and its key processes to deliver on the strategic breakthrough objectives that are proposed as part of the Hoshin planning process.

The concept of daily management defined in TQM is a completely new component of planning at DCCC. In the past, units gathered the data that suited their individually perceived purposes and needs. Units tended to gather two types of data: data required by various regulatory agencies or funding sources and data required for internal reporting. Unfortunately, these types of data do little to promote process improvement. One result of the implementation of daily management is an administrative fundamentals document that sets forth each unit's mission; customers; key processes; process suppliers, steps, outputs; and data elements that measure the quality characteristics of key processes. By showing how units are connected to one another as internal suppliers and customers, the document facilitates the emergence of cross-functional teams to work on processes that flow across departmental boundaries.

Total Staff Involvement. Hoshin planning requires input from all levels of staff before, during, and after the creation of the strategic plan. Once the strategic plan has been formulated, each unit develops an annual plan targeted to achieving the breakthrough objectives outlined in the organization's strategic plan. Hoshin planning generates extensive involvement across departments as the strategic plan is deployed throughout the organization and translated into unit action plans.

Many members of the DCCC community viewed its strategic plan for the 1980s as belonging primarily to the planning office, the president and his cabinet, and the board of trustees. The executive staff communicated the plan to staff, but they were not involved extensively in providing input that affected its character. By contrast, we based the strategic plan for the 1990s largely on input from the people who work at DCCC.

Continuous Communication. *Catch ball* is an important term in Hoshin planning. It refers to the frequent communication that takes place, both vertically and horizontally, as the planning process unfolds. Top management communicates the organizational vision and the strategic plan developed from internal and external stakeholders' input. Departmental units respond with the plans that they develop to achieve breakthrough progress toward the strategic objectives of the organization. Periodic review and negotiation take place, with the twofold goals of ensuring, first, that the departmental plans are sufficient to meet the goals and aligned with the vision and, second, that the plans are not beyond the capabilities of the organization. This continuous communication identifies the places where training is needed and where duplication of effort, clashing priorities, or unexpected internal or external events have made renegotiation necessary. Catch ball keeps employees at all levels focused on where the organization is going and on how individual units contribute to the effort. As the organization internalizes the vision, units become better aligned with the vision. This alignment facilitates the conservation of resources for high-priority activities.

Implications of Daily Management

In 1991, we instituted daily management in all administrative departments and offices at DCCC. Each office developed a mission statement, identified and flowcharted the key processes, and developed a data collection plan that could be used to monitor the efficiency of the process steps and the effectiveness of the process outputs. Daily management and TQM tie into the strategic plan on two levels: First, the strategic plan commits DCCC to using TQM in pursuing all its goals for the 1990s. Second, one goal for the 1990s is the implementation of TQM.

A total quality (TQ) steering group now supports implementation of daily management at the college. In 1992, the TQ group identified the benefits and obstacles of implementation from the perspective of administrative staff at the college. The steering group used a TQ tool, the affinity diagram, to organize the qualitative data gathered from staff into thematic areas. The obstacles fell into five major categories: competing demands and time constraints, training, communication and recognition, consistency between philosophy and actions and interdepartmental issues, and external complexities. The TQ steering group constructed tree diagrams to identify potential methods of removing these obstacles. (Brassard, 1989, describes affinity and tree diagrams.) The diagrams suggested several high-leverage activities that would remove several other obstacles as well. For example, the tree diagram for training indicated that one method is to create a pool of internal coaches or mentors who can assist anyone struggling with a particular method or tool. This approach addresses many of the needs expressed by staff related to content, length, style, and delivery of training. It also addresses one of the time constraints commonly cited—staff cannot get away for blocks of workshop training—and it provides the mentor with recognition for the skills that he or she has learned.

Input from DCCC staff is also making clear that training needs are shifting from our usual teach-and-practice workshops to workshops that serve as drop-in clinics. The move to clinics is high leverage because it better serves the needs of internal customers and because it requires less time and fewer resources to prepare and conduct. Another activity that has evolved is a TQ cooperative that support staff have established for themselves. The cooperative is an opportunity for support staff to learn more about TQ, to hear TQ examples from their peers, and to communicate their concerns and problems with TQ. A liaison now exists between the coop founders and the TQ steering group. This liaison provides the steering group with input from a key customer group, and it has become a vehicle for communication, recognition, and training among support staff.

References

Brassard, M. *The Memory Jogger Plus: Featuring the Seven Management and Planning Tools.* Methuen, Mass.: GOAL/QPC, 1989.

GOAL/QPC Research Committee. *Hoshin Planning: A Planning System for Implementing Total Quality Management (TQM).* Methuen, Mass.: GOAL/QPC, 1989.

King, B. *Hoshin Planning: The Developmental Approach.* Methuen, Mass.: GOAL/QPC, 1989.

MARY ANN HEVERLY *is director of institutional research at Delaware County Community College, Media, Pennsylvania.*

JEROME S. PARKER *is dean of management systems and planning at Delaware County Community College.*

*Several types of facilitators emerge as teams work to improve
processes: the delegator, the director, the workhorse, and the
cheerleader. Different styles can affect team learning.*

The Role of the Facilitator on
Total Quality Management Teams

William L. (Lindy) Eakin

At The University of Kansas (KU), we are discovering various approaches to
team facilitation, and we are learning about it and team behavior. Our teams
include a team leader who is the manager-supervisor in charge of the
process, five to six team members involved with the process, and a facilitator. The administrator responsible for the process is the team sponsor. The
facilitator is the Total Quality Management (TQM) expert who helps the
team and team leader use TQM tools and keep the group functioning. The
facilitator, who is knowledgeable about the tools and techniques of TQM,
encourages team members to participate and simply facilitates the process.
Before activating pilot TQM project teams, team leaders and facilitators
completed training concerning the roles and responsibilities of team leader,
facilitator, and members; a problem-solving model to guide teams in improving processes; use of TQM tools and methods; and group dynamics and
organizational behavior.

The Problem-Solving Model

At KU, the process follows the basic structure of continuous process
improvement: understand the process, characterize the process, simplify
the process, and, if successful, institutionalize the changes. The plan-do-
check-act cycle is built into the model. Each team decides how to apply the
tools to the particular circumstances of the process that it is improving. The
basic tools and techniques of flowcharting, cause-and-effect diagrams, data
collection, solution generation, and testing are used, but the order depends
on the circumstances of the process under study. The facilitator, as the TQM

expert, is expected to help guide the team in the selection of appropriate tools at the appropriate times.

The Facilitator

Team facilitators generally are outsiders, that is, they are not staff directly involved in the process to be improved. This fact lends objectivity to their role as experts and helps them to facilitate group processes. Four facilitation models emerged from our experiences over the past year.

The Delegator. The delegator plays a low-key role on the team after using a case study to introduce the team to the problem-solving model. The facilitator helps delegate the usage of tools, determination of tasks, and general activity during the meetings to team members. For instance, the tasks of setting up the meeting, taking minutes, drawing process diagrams, gathering data, providing documentation, and leading discussion are assigned to various team members. These responsibilities are assigned at the beginning of each meeting, and they are rotated among members. The facilitator maintains an active role by helping the team answer such questions as these: Where do we go from here? Have we collected enough data? When do we get to solutions? The facilitator maintains this delegating posture except when an occasion arises that requires the facilitator to clarify the process, move on to the next step, or articulate the group consensus. The delegation approach fosters ownership of the process and outcome among team members. It builds team members' confidence in their ability to use a problem-solving model, and the experience deepens their understanding of the principles of TQM.

The Director. In the director role, the facilitator is much more visible. The approach is didactic, and the facilitator plays a teaching role on the team. Each step of the problem-solving model is an opportunity to review and elicit discussion on the next step in the model and the purposes of the steps. The team leader convenes the meetings and assigns tasks, such as taking minutes, producing copies of flowcharts, and collecting data. The director-facilitator acts as the TQM teacher. The director helps team members think through what they are doing and why by asking such questions as What happens here? and Why do we do it this way?

The Workhorse. As the name implies, the workhorse tends to do much of the work related to the use of TQM tools. In this role, the facilitator may take the minutes of the meeting, work at the flip chart, convert the flowchart into computer software, analyze data, and assume other tasks to spare the team leader and team members from the effort. At the same time, the workhorse serves as a resource person and facilitator for the team. This role reduces learning opportunities for other team members.

The Cheerleader. The cheerleader model places the emphasis on social interaction. In this role, the facilitator helps create an atmosphere of excitement and good feelings about being involved with the team. The cheerleader is especially skillful at drawing team members out and at facilitating interaction. Being sociable helps reduce some tension among team members who are less committed to the project or who suspect a hidden agenda. Reduced tension allows the team leader to be more directive and establishes the facilitator as a nonthreatening presence who can serve as resource person without raising concern about motives.

Lessons Learned

Training. The experiences gained in facilitating teams provide several lessons. First and foremost, team members should be exposed to the concepts and principles of TQM before they ever serve on a team. On at least two of our teams, all team members participated in a two-day workshop on the principles of TQM. This background gave them an understanding of why the teams are formed, what they intend to accomplish, management's commitment to TQM, and the revolution in management philosophy that is part of TQM.

Team Identity. Team identity and cohesiveness are important. Early in the process, the facilitator and the team leader should discuss the importance of teamwork. They need to examine ways to develop and enhance the identity of the team so that all team members have ownership of the effort and the process. At the first meeting of my team, the person taking minutes (who was using a supplied form) asked about the name of the team (the form had a place for team name). After discussing several ideas, the team reached consensus on a name. At the next meeting, one team member provided us with buttons bearing the team name. We wore the buttons with pride.

Sharing Knowledge. We hold occasional meetings of team leaders and facilitators to share experiences. By comparing experiences and sharing tips—simple things, such as changing the seating arrangements to alter team interaction—we reassure everyone that situations are not unique. Rotating turns at the flip chart draws reluctant team members into the process and shifts the focus of responsibility from the team leader or facilitator to the team members.

The Outsider. One element in the process by which we match teams and facilitators is the conscious choice of a facilitator who is not involved in the process that is to be improved. Such a position allows the facilitator to act as an objective outsider who can ask dumb questions about the process without being threatening. This posture is particularly useful in flowcharting. Employees often assume that everyone knows the process in detail, or they are so familiar with the process that they do not examine it at a sufficiently basic level. The facilitator can pose questions in a nonthreatening rather than challenging way: "Why do you do that?" is challenging. "What do you do next?" is not.

An Expert. The presence of the facilitator as the TQM expert is critical. Even with an introduction to TQM principles and tools, team members need a resident expert who can assure them that they are using the tools correctly or that their measures for data collection are appropriate. Perhaps more important, the facilitator ensures that the team does not shortchange the process improvement model. Teams have a pronounced tendency to jump to solutions immediately upon finding a problem in the flowcharting or data collection stage. The facilitator can act as a conscience that helps the team to stick with the problem-solving model from start to finish. The facilitator also helps the team leader or other team members from exercising judgment over suggestions during brainstorming and assures that individuals do not dominate the discussion.

Barriers. At least two of our teams expressed the belief that the process chosen for improvement did not have a problem. The teams saw their processes as already streamlined and as being as efficient as possible. Several team meetings made it clear to them how TQM could help them understand their process and thus improve it. The predisposition to feel that there is no problem can be a major obstacle. For that reason, the team leader and the facilitator must succeed in promoting discussion in the initial stages and earn the trust of the team. Simply asserting that there is a problem creates an adversarial relationship and makes team members defensive about their process. The facilitator must communicate that one does not have to be sick in order to get better, and the team needs to believe that there is value in what it is doing. The flip side is that asking production workers for their opinions about how they do their jobs is a tremendous boost for morale. All too often, the job is defined either by a supervisor who used to do it and now insists that it be done a certain way or by a supervisor who, although he or she has never done the work, knows best how to do it. Staff involvement is a major boost to morale.

One hurdle that teams must overcome is the conflict between the time spent in team meetings and the time that team members must spend carrying out their daily responsibilities. Team members generally expressed concern at the first meeting about the amount of time that participation on the team would require. However, by the time they began making progress in understanding their process, flowcharting, and collecting data, most team members committed to the principles of TQM and to using the tools to improve their daily work.

Time constraints can have positive consequences. One team worked on the telephone reception process in the department of human resources. Since team members are responsible for answering phone calls, routing callers, and providing answers, management took over the phones during team meetings. Team members were satisfied when this experience helped their bosses acquire a better appreciation of the demands that they faced.

Another team is studying the voucher audit process—essentially the bill-paying section of the comptroller's office. They suspended team activities to close the fiscal year as the seasonal demands of the office took precedence over the team. However, they returned eagerly to team meetings after a two-month hiatus.

The facilitator role has hazards as well as benefits. One facilitator became too involved with his team and developed ownership of the process. At one team meeting, he proudly presented his revision of one of the forms used in the process. The team members, wanting to solve their own problems, took offense at his intrusion into their process. The team leader visited with the facilitator after the team meeting to address the good intentions that had undermined the team dynamics.

Senior Management. I served as facilitator for a team in the comptroller's office, which may be unusual because the comptroller reports to me. Certainly, my position influenced team dynamics, but by making time to meet each week and by demonstrating a commitment to a new management style, I emphasized my commitment to TQM to staff and middle management. Extra effort is necessary for a senior administrator to get the team to take charge and ownership of the process, but playing the dumb outsider helped me to overcome my position of authority relative to the team.

Leadership by example is a potent signal. Resources must be committed to the education and training of employees. Employees must receive release time to participate in teams and implement the improvements that have been recommended. The commitment of our own time—the most valuable personal resource—and our participation on a team clearly demonstrate our commitment to quality and continuous improvement.

WILLIAM L. (LINDY) EAKIN *is associate vice chancellor for administration and finance at The University of Kansas, Lawrence.*

Focus groups can supplement traditional survey research to identify customer needs and examine critical processes.

Using Focus Groups to Clarify Customer Needs

Mary M. Sapp, M. Lewis Temares

Survey research is often used to gather data about the needs of students and other groups on campus. However, traditional surveys are limited, because the questions and the range of potential answers are set in advance, and respondents are limited to the topics covered by the survey. Moreover, surveys emphasize questions that can be answered via rating scales or a closed set of responses, as opposed to open-ended and interactive questions.

Focus groups provide an effective complement to traditional surveys. A focus group is a small (six- to twelve-member), relatively homogenous group that meets with the help of a trained moderator in a nonthreatening, relaxed environment for a 90- to 120-minute discussion about a selected topic (Bers and Smith, 1990). Using focus groups allows for group interaction, increases insight into the reasons why certain opinions are held, and is capable of providing in-depth information about the needs, interests, and concerns of participants.

Focus Group Methodology

An excellent literature on focus group methodology has developed over the past few years (Bers, 1989; Bers and Smith, 1990; Brodigan, 1992; Krueger, 1988; McLaughlin and Snyder, 1990; Merton, Fiske, and Kendall, 1990; Morgan, 1988). These materials deal with such considerations as developing the questions, selecting the participants, selecting and setting up the site, selecting the moderators, conducting the discussion, and writing the reports. As with all research tools, a foundation in the underlying principles is essential to assure appropriate application.

Student Life Focus Groups

To supplement the University of Miami's annual strategic planning process, the president in 1990 charged seven issues task forces with the responsibility for analyzing needs in such areas as curriculum, faculty productivity and rewards, facilities, and student life. One of these groups, the Student Life Issues Task Force, was presented with the results of past surveys of enrolled students, graduating seniors, and withdrawing students; retention studies; and other existing institutional research dealing with student life. The group identified several areas that needed more analysis: advising, career planning, counseling services, extracurricular activities, residential colleges, and support services. In early 1991, the office of planning and institutional research conducted focus groups to probe the nature of student needs and concerns in each of these areas.

Findings

Although previous surveys had determined general levels of student satisfaction, the focus groups were able to probe why students felt as they did. For example, students indicated a need for more peer counselors (as opposed to professional counselors), since resident assistants, whom the university views as a source of peer counseling, are sometimes seen more as "police" than as counselors. Students volunteered that communication about extracurricular activities should be improved and that school spirit was lacking. They also said that commuter students had a special need for activities.

Students liked the university's residential college concept but volunteered a list of suggestions relating to security, maintenance, mail delivery, and laundry facilities. Such observations would have been difficult to elicit from paper-and-pencil surveys. One advantage of focus group discussions is that they allow students to volunteer their areas of concern.

The offices of student account services and financial aid had been aware that satisfaction was low for their areas, but they attributed the dissatisfaction to the students' inability to get more money. Focus groups showed that the complexity of their procedures and the lack of communication and coordination were sources of dissatisfaction. In particular, students did not like being sent across campus from one office to another to rectify problems with their financial aid. Special reports summarizing the nature of student concerns were prepared for these offices.

Summaries of the student life focus group findings also were used by the task force on residential colleges, which was established later in 1991 to help determine the effect of residential colleges on student retention and recruitment. Given the success of the student life focus groups, the task force on residential colleges decided to conduct its own focus groups to explore student attitudes regarding on-campus housing in general and residential colleges in particular.

Results

Recommendations from the Student Life Issues Task Force led to a variety of changes. For example, in response to the focus group's expressed need for peer counseling, a peer facilitator program was piloted in one of the residential colleges this past year. Students interested in becoming peer facilitators were trained to respond to problems experienced by fellow students. We retained this program, and it will be expanded to the other residential colleges. A new student group called Alma Mater was established to improve school spirit. Moreover, we appointed a director of commuter student affairs to coordinate commuter student activities, including dissemination of information to commuter students.

We improved security in the residential colleges by installing a card access system, and changes have been made to maintenance, mail delivery, and laundry facilities in the residential colleges. The Office of Financial Assistance Services opened a satellite office near the Student Account Services Office in order to improve communication and coordination between them. Student reaction is very positive. A computerized telephone system that will allow students to check on the status of financial aid processing is under development.

Conclusion

Traditional surveys are a valuable tool for institutional researchers and others gathering data to support quality improvement programs. Focus groups offer another technique for understanding the needs and opinions of members of the university community by probing selected areas of special interest. By improving our understanding of actual needs, we become better able to improve the quality of services to students.

References

Bers, T. "The Popularity and Problems of Focus-Group Research." *College and University: The Journal of AACRAO,* 1989, *64,* 260–268.

Bers, T., and Smith, K. "A Primer for Practitioners: Focus Group Research." Paper presented at conference of the Association for Institutional Research, Louisville, Kentucky, 1990.

Brodigan, D. "Focus Group Interviews: Applications for Institutional Research." *AIR Professional File,* 1992, *43.*

Krueger, R. A. *Focus Groups: A Practical Guide for Applied Research.* Newbury Park, Calif.: Sage, 1988.

McLaughlin, G., and Snyder, J. "Points for Consideration for Focus Group Interviews." *IRPA Volume 90–91,* 1990, *8.*

Merton, R. K., Fiske, M., and Kendall, P. L. *The Focused Interview: A Manual of Problems and Procedures.* New York: Free Press, 1990.
Morgan, D. L. *Focus Groups as Qualitative Research.* Newbury Park, Calif.: Sage, 1988.

MARY M. SAPP is director of planning and institutional research at the University of Miami, Coral Gables, Florida.

M. LEWIS TEMARES is vice president for information resources at the University of Miami.

Total Quality Management tools promote understanding of the way things happen.

Using Total Quality Management Tools to Improve Organizational Wellness

Sharon Koberna, Pam Walter

Total Quality Management (TQM) offers a wide variety of tools for process improvement. Rio Salado Community College applies the tools for four main purposes: meeting facilitation, process definition, project selection, and data gathering and analysis. Not only are these tools used by formal continuous improvement teams (CITs), but they also are being applied increasingly in meetings, planning, decision making, and problem solving by operational units throughout the college.

Meeting Facilitation

Because TQM increased the frequency with which employees participated in meetings, we adopted several tools to increase meeting effectiveness and maximize productivity. The ground rules model is used to set the meeting environment and establish the context for interaction among participants. The ground rules include such items as *no rank in the room, listen as an ally,* and *everyone participates, no one dominates.* These rules are agreed on by those in the group, and they govern the interactions of members during meetings.

The issue bin is written on a flip chart and posted in plain view during the meeting. When topics or issues arise that are important but not pertinent to the topic under discussion, they are written on the flip chart to be addressed later. This technique helps to keep the discussion on track and ensures that important thoughts are not lost.

A plus/delta evaluation is completed at the end of each meeting. It identifies areas that made the session successful (pluses) and areas that need improvement (deltas). This technique provides the leader, the recorder, and other members of the team with direct feedback. The information gained in the plus/delta evaluation is used to make improvements for the next meeting.

Process Definition

When a process is identified for improvement, the first challenge is to define all its components so that we have a clear picture of what it entails. The affinity diagram is a structured form of brainstorming. It is very useful as an initial step to group large amounts of complex and apparently unrelated information in meaningful ways. It allows the group to identify patterns and relationships among the many components of a process. We used this tool to help identify the essential components of large processes, such as student program advisement and class schedule development.

The fishbone (cause-and-effect) diagram allows the group to further define the components of a process by relating them to outcomes. It segregates the information into logical categories and graphically illustrates relationships between problems and their causes. Groups found this tool to be very helpful in identifying a focus for improvement efforts in such processes as textbook distribution, mailing, and printing.

To illustrate the sequence of steps and individuals involved in a process, a deployment flowchart is often used. The chart, a diagram of the steps in a process, identifies the person or function involved in each step and applicable quality issues that impact each step. It also includes a time line. The flowchart is extremely helpful in revealing areas of rework and nonproductive process steps. Often, completing the chart enables the group to identify the source or sources of the process problem. Such processes as unrecovered student debt and internal requisition processing were improved using this tool.

Project Selection

After using the appropriate process definition tools, the group is sometimes faced with several alternatives from which to choose in improving the process. To assist in selection, the N/3 method or the straw voting method of prioritization is often used. Both methods require the members to vote until consensus is reached on project selection. Both methods are effective in moving a group forward when its members seem deadlocked on an issue.

Force field analysis is another tool used in project selection. It helps to identify the forces that could either promote (driving forces) or inhibit (restraining forces) the completion of a project or implementation of a change. It allows the group to evaluate the feasibility of an action objectively, to anticipate potential problems, and to develop strategies for dealing with them.

Data Gathering and Analysis

Numerous charts and graphs are used to present and analyze data visually. Histograms, bar charts, Pareto charts, and run charts are used when appropriate, and they are often easier to understand than are columns and tables of numbers. Histograms, bar charts, and Pareto charts often clearly indicate a focus for change and provide direction for selecting the area in which change will have the greatest impact.

Figure 15.1—Pareto charts—shows how we use these tools within Rio Salado for a variety of purposes. Although Rio employees are knowledgeable in the use of all these tools, several are used more often than others. As the two charts indicate, ground rules, issue bin, and plus/delta evaluation are

Figure 15.1. Use of TQM Tools at Rio Salado

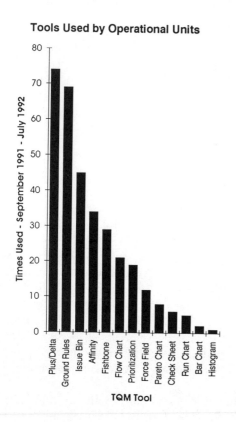

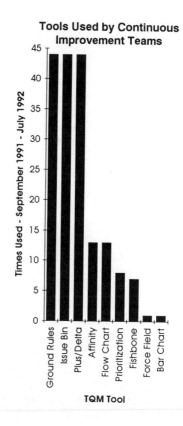

used the most often. These tools are very successful in structuring and managing meetings, and almost every meeting by CITs and other areas of the college includes them.

Both CITs and operational units often use the affinity diagram to identify the components of processes. The operational units use the fishbone (cause-and-effect) diagram more often than the CITs, while the CITs make greater use of the flowchart to define processes. The fishbone can be applied to a wide variety of topics, and the operational units often use it in a less structured format for many purposes.

The emphasis on use of TQM tools for process definition rather than data gathering and analysis is probably due to the college's new focus on processes. As processes are examined, it is becoming clear that many function as the result of some mysterious "miracle factor":

step 1 → step 2 → "a miracle happens" → process complete

Many existing processes have not been documented, which means that there is a strong emphasis on process description, process development, or both.

As the charts indicate, operational units use a wider variety of tools for data gathering and analysis than the continuous improvement teams do. One explanation for this finding is the nature of the processes currently under examination by the CITs and the fact that several are not yet at the data-gathering and analysis step of the continuous improvement cycle. As more CITs move closer to gathering data and as more processes are examined throughout the college, the use of tools for data gathering and analysis will probably increase.

Pitfalls

We find that many groups have a common problem when they use the tools just described: They tend to discuss and evaluate ideas before it is appropriate to do so. It is important for the TQM facilitator to guide the group away from discussions that interfere with effective use of the tools.

One problem that often surfaces when groups use the deployment flowchart is the desire to jump to premature conclusions about ways of improving a process or solving a problem before it is clearly defined or data are gathered. To counteract this tendency, several groups use a solution bin in which possible solutions are placed until the appropriate time. This practice seems to allay fears that good ideas will be lost, and it allows the group to keep on track. Again, the TQM facilitator is instrumental in keeping the group focused on the process and moving through the continuous improvement cycle.

Because many processes at the college have not been defined clearly, the flowchart is the most difficult tool for groups to use. Charting a process requires knowledge of the steps in it, and in many cases these steps are not clear. Several charts must sometimes be completed before a process can be illustrated clearly. Often, a group is tempted to flowchart the process as it should be, not as it actually operates. Since the end result of a process is known, we find it helpful in these cases to work from the end result backward to the beginning of the process. Often, it is necessary to involve people outside of the original group in the process of constructing the chart. This fact emphasizes the importance of including all the key people involved in a process on the CIT or in the group, even if their inclusion is ad hoc.

Benefits

One of the challenges that formal continuous improvement teams and operational units often face is clearly defining the way things happen and determining the best way of implementing and measuring process improvement. Rio Salado found that one of the greatest benefits of using the TQM tools and techniques is process identification, definition, and documentation.

As formal CITs and other groups meet to solve problems and improve processes, the interaction often bogs down in lengthy discussions that do not result in a clear direction or focus for the group's efforts. We found that use of the tools clarifies the major issues and depersonalizes the problem, which allows the group to move forward.

Another benefit derived from the use of the tools, particularly the flowchart, is that people became increasingly aware of the college as a system of interconnected units. Appreciation of how actions taken by one area can affect other areas in the college is growing. Moreover, communication and cooperation are increasing as people work together on cross-functional teams to improve collegewide processes.

As the Pareto charts in Figure 15.1 illustrate, the use of the TQM tools is not confined to formal continuous improvement teams. Throughout the college, we use the tools at all levels in planning, problem solving, and decision making. The tools give us a means for integrating the concepts of total quality into everyday operations, and they are enhancing Rio Salado's movement toward a quality organization.

SHARON KOBERNA is TQM coordinator at Rio Salado Community College, Phoenix, Arizona.

PAM WALTER is institutional research coordinator at Rio Salado Community College.

Total Quality Management reduces the time spent on a complex data collection and reporting process by 40 percent.

Simplifying a Process with Flowcharts

JoAnn M. Williams

The University of Kansas is one of approximately fifty institutions participating in a five-year study to analyze doctoral applicants and students in a sample set of departments. As the programmer in the Office of Institutional Research and Planning (OIRP) responsible for preparing the data for the project, I found the process to be a complex and time-consuming task. The required data are maintained in a variety of offices and in both paper and computer formats. My task is to collect and format to specifications all required data, ensure data consistency and integrity, and transmit the data to the agency conducting the analyses on behalf of the participating institutions. After the second year of the study, I made a flowchart of the process to look for ways in which data collection could be improved.

Data Collection Process

Figure 16.1, a condensed version of the original twenty-two page flowchart, tracks the flow of this process:

Step 1 writes computer programs to extract the data required for the applicant and enrolled student files from the student records information system (SRIS).

Step 2 downloads and imports these data into a microcomputer data base. At this point, less than half of the data for the two files—applicants and enrolled students—has been collected. The remainder of the data is collected from the human resources management system (HRMS), the departments, the graduate school, the Office of Financial Aid, and systems development. There are thirty-six variables for enrolled students and twenty-seven applicant variables. Seventeen data items covering personal information (six items), test scores (two items), past and present degree information

Figure 16.1. Condensed Flowchart of the Data Collection Process

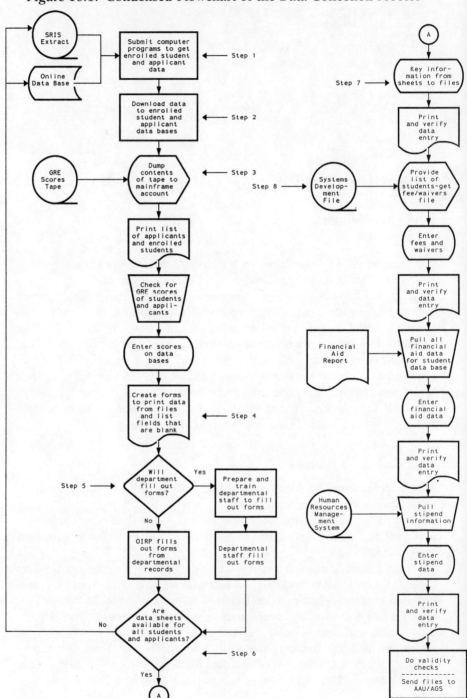

(five items), and financial information (four items) are common to both enrolled students and applicants.

Step 3 extracts graduate record exam (GRE) scores from magnetic tape. (They are not available from SRIS.) I check each person on the applicant and enrolled student lists against a machine-readable file of the GRE scores by matching on social security number, name, or birth date. I record scores, when found, on paper and then enter them on the appropriate data base. Many of the student and applicant scores cannot be found in the GRE file.

Step 4 uses information extracted from the data bases to generate forms on which the remaining data maintained in paper files in the academic departments can be recorded.

Step 5 gives departments two options: They can complete the forms for their applicants and enrolled students, or they can allow OIRP to collect the data from their own internal records. Three departments chose the first option, and two chose the second.

Step 6 enters the data into the data bases and checks them for accuracy.

Step 7 backtracks to collect information about students enrolled in or applied to the Ph.D. program in the study who have not appeared on the other lists.

Step 8 generates and verifies the remaining data from the three sources displayed in Figure 16.1.

Improvements

This long and complex process needed improvement. Figure 16.2 is a skeletal view of the steps in the new process together with an explanation of the associated improvements.

Evaluation

I reduced the time spent collecting the data for fall 1991 students and applicants by more than 40 percent from the time spent for fall 1990. This figure does not include the time saved by department personnel, who did not code data sheets the second year. A portion of the time saved can be attributed directly to the learning curve associated with any repetitive project. However, by constructing a flowchart of the process I was able to "see" changes that would improve the process immensely and immediately.

Hints

A flowchart depicts a process as it actually happens by visualizing the steps in the process. I found it helpful to make a flowchart of the data collection and reporting process from beginning to end. However, for some complex tasks, it may be beneficial to concentrate on one particular part of the

Figure 16.2. Improving the Flow of the Data Collection Process

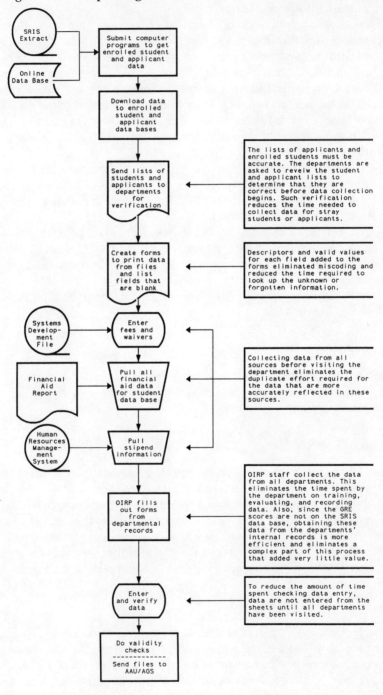

process. Flowchart construction can be time-consuming and tedious, but it also is a systematic way to uncover sensible solutions that have significant payoffs.

JoAnn M. Williams *is a research analyst in the Office of Institutional Research and Planning at The University of Kansas, Lawrence.*

Formal documentation of team activities and solutions can promote communication and understanding of continuous improvement achievements.

Documenting Total Quality Management Projects

Pam Walter

Project documentation is the final step in Rio Salado's continuous improvement cycle (CIC). This documentation is very important because it assists others in understanding the work that the team has done, and it documents in detail when, where, how, and why we made process changes.

The continuous improvement team (CIT) prepares two documents: the final report and the project storyboard. The final report is a detailed account of the team's improvement efforts, including background information about the need for the project and the identification and reasons for selecting the particular team members. It describes the work of the team at each step in the CIC, and it discusses the Total Quality Management (TQM) tools used. It includes histograms, bar charts, or Pareto charts presenting the data both before and after implementing changes. The project statement and flowcharts of the process under study before and after the changes are also included.

The final report also describes the control systems put into place to ensure that the change is permanent. Additionally, actions are taken to ensure that the change implemented during the project is reviewed periodically for appropriateness.

Experience taught us that ongoing documentation by CITs is essential for the final report drawn up at the conclusion of a project. Due to the length of time required for measuring the effect of a change—generally six to nine months—a good deal of the group memory is lost without regular documentation. The first CIT to complete its work and begin documentation learned this lesson the hard way. The members could not remember why they had completed three deployment flowcharts or in what order. The team had not dated the flip chart sheets with the results of group brainstorming, affinity diagrams, and cause-and-effect diagrams, and it did not trace a number of details in the process.

To deal with this problem and to facilitate the preparation of accurate and complete final reports, we developed work sheets for the following eight topics: evaluation criteria for project selection, project statement, customer expectations, data types, data collection, change implementation, change standardization, and ensuring the life of the change. Each CIT designates one member to serve as recorder, and it is that person's responsibility to prepare complete and accurate records of the team's efforts. Minutes are sent to the TQM coordinator after each CIT meeting so that the progress of all CITs can be monitored.

In addition to the final report, the team prepares a project storyboard, an abbreviated version of the final report containing an entry for each step in the continuous improvement cycle. It is usually presented on a large piece of poster board and provides a view of the team's accomplishments at a glance.

To ensure quality and consistency, Rio's information processing center uses a standard format and style to prepare the reports and text for the storyboards. We created major headings for the storyboard in two-color format. Every team uses the same headings.

Accurate and complete project documentation is essential to provide a written record of the CIT's thought processes and efforts. If the same process or a similar one is examined at a future time, good documentation can help prevent duplication of effort. The report documents the reasons for the process changes and compiles all the pertinent information about the project into one document.

After completing the project documentation, members of the continuous improvement team present their report and storyboard to the college's TQM strategic planning steering team. All project reports are filed in the TQM coordinator's office, and they are available for any employee to review. Later CITs used the reports of their predecessors as a guide in developing their own documentation.

The storyboards are posted in hallways and meeting rooms to give employees an opportunity to review the accomplishments of the CITs. When members of the college give presentations about Rio Salado's TQM program, they display the storyboard and use it as a guide in explaining the CIC and the functions of CITs.

Although the complete documentation is valuable, it does not come without a cost. The project report and the storyboard take time to complete and assemble. Generally a CIT subcommittee is formed to develop the documentation. The entire team reviews the first draft and the complete report. This process requires three to four additional meetings, and it can add four weeks or more to the time required for completion of the CIC.

Having the information processing center maintain the standard format expedites the process as well as having the final reports from other CITs on file for reference.

PAM WALTER is institutional research coordinator at Rio Salado Community College, Phoenix, Arizona.

PART FOUR

Organizing for Total Quality Management

After the president commits to adopt a quality improvement
process, what does one do?

On Your Mark, Get Set, Go!

Robert S. Winter

On October 31, 1991, leaders of the University of Illinois at Chicago (UIC)
met at the annual chancellor's retreat to discuss the concepts of Total Quality
Management (TQM) and examine the way in which they might be applied
to the campus. The next day, the retreat concluded with a commitment from
the chancellor to explore the adoption of quality management at UIC on a
pilot basis. Soon after, we took a number of actions to get the program under
way: The chancellor appointed me coordinator of the pilot program. I
formed the Quality Improvement Work Group (QIWG) to assist with the
design process. Senior management selected academic affairs, administrative affairs, research, student affairs, business affairs, the library, the college
of business administration, and the eye and ear infirmary to develop quality
improvement teams in the initial phase of the program. The chancellor
established the Quality Improvement Task Force (QITF), representing
managers and leaders, which met for the first time in February 1992.

The opportunity to have an impact on the organization was extraordinary, but I responded particularly to the chancellor's compelling reason for
this important initiative: The university would become more humane
through the adoption of quality management processes by treating employees with respect and caring, and it would improve the overall quality of life
at the university.

I was not new to this field. After hearing Lawrence A. Sherr, Chancellors
Club Teaching Professor and professor of business administration at The
University of Kansas, at the annual forum of the Association for Institutional
Research in 1989, I became a student of quality management principles and
practices. Yet when faced with an opportunity to implement this process, I
was not certain what the logical steps would be.

NEW DIRECTIONS FOR INSTITUTIONAL RESEARCH, no. 78, Summer 1993 © Jossey-Bass Publishers

101

I read about what others were doing. The materials can be classified into two categories: publications that describe specific quality management processes implemented at various institutions and publications that describe the conditions necessary to adopt these processes successfully (for example, obtain commitment from top management). Goals and diagnostics were helpful but insufficient. Although I understood how other organizations had evolved, I did not have a road map that would help me to prepare a comprehensive plan for the adoption of a quality management process at UIC.

Initial Issues and Questions

Administrative Behavior. The first challenge that I faced was my own behavior. I was trapped between the urge to assume direct leadership and guide the adoption of the quality management process personally and the critical principle of quality management that focuses on participatory processes. In an effort to overcome that tendency, I looked for expert assistance among my colleagues. I was fortunate to find other individuals at UIC who had been reading about and in some cases applying principles of quality management. We became the work group.

Networking. Colleagues from other colleges and universities provided me with moral and technical support. However, I needed to find a local network. In Chicago, I discovered several important connections: the Chicago Quality Council, which is composed of a few leading companies, including Motorola and Sprint, and the local chapters of the Association for Quality and Participation and the American Society for Quality Control.

Scope. Based on discussions held during the chancellor's retreat and with the deans, we decided to focus initially on administrative units.

Terminology. Most campus leaders believed that UIC was yielding to a fad. Terminology is particularly problematic, so we adopted the term *quality improvement* (QI) in preference to *total quality management*. At present, we use the term *quality advancement*.

Infrastructure. To ensure the participation of those with a direct and immediate impact on the adoption process, we identified three basic groups: top management, the QITF, and the QIWG. Subsequently we added two more: the facilitators team and the leaders team.

More Issues and Questions

Commitment. Both the literature and our own instincts underscored that it was imperative for top management both to be involved in and to demonstrate commitment to the quality improvement process. Decisions made at that level affect policies and procedures across the institution, and they have a profound impact on the organization's climate. For example, the process used to reduce the budget sends a message to employees. The choice between a process to manage attrition and retrain employees, on the one hand, and layoffs, on the other, indicates how an organization values its employees. Although the chancellor demonstrated his support and interest in QI, others did not invest much of their time and effort in the process. Getting these leaders involved in and excited about QI is my challenge. A critical component of their education is their participation in executive programs dealing with the philosophy and principles of QI.

Agenda. The initial charge to members of the QITF asked them to develop a UIC perspective on QI by identifying common definitions, objectives, and values; develop a process to evaluate the impact of the QI teams; establish a process to communicate the progress of pilot teams; and establish an employee recognition program. The chancellor did not appoint a chairperson for the QITF because the members needed to establish ownership of the group. I chaired the group by default for the first two meetings. Since then, the chair serves on a rotating basis.

The chancellor charged the QIWG to develop plans encouraging the use of team concepts and principles, to strengthen and complement the training programs, and to support the QITF by researching the literature on QI concepts and tools. We established a work group of team facilitators and leaders for three reasons: Their input is critical in the design of training programs, their meetings facilitate networking among teams and team members, and their shared experiences lead to improved processes.

Training. What types of training should be provided, by whom, and for whom? Top management, the members of the QITF and the QIWG, middle managers, leaders and facilitators, team members, and staff supporting the adoption process all need to be educated in the principles and concepts of QI and to develop a working knowledge of the tools. It is imperative for the training programs to be congruent with participants' interests. For example, it is inappropriate to expose top management initially to technical details. Their interests are policy based with a focus on organizational implications. In contrast, team members need to understand the philosophical foundations of QI, but the emphasis of training must be on team building and problem-solving processes and tools.

We established four training programs: (1) Basic Concepts of QI, a one-day workshop for managers and members of task forces, which focuses on the principles and concepts of QI. (2) Leader-Facilitator Training, a two-and-a-half-day workshop for leaders, facilitators, and middle managers, which reviews the processes and tools used by QI teams. (3) Team Member Training, a one-day orientation workshop for team members, which establishes meeting ground rules, discusses principles, and helps team members to gain a general understanding of QI processes and tools. And (4) Leadership Training, a one-day orientation workshop, which supplies leaders and facilitators with information about team-building activities and troubleshooting.

Organizational Transformation. After designing the training programs, we developed a plan to guide the transformation of the university into a quality organization. The literature identifies four stages of cultural transformation that are common to most organizations but that differ from setting to setting in their length and overlap. At UIC, we identified four distinct stages. *Stage 1:* Create awareness in the university community about the QI process and provide opportunities for training and organizing for quality. *Stage 2:* Establish initial teams, provide appropriate training and logistical support, develop employee recognition programs, and design communication systems. *Stage 3:* Adopt the QI process by establishing an infrastructure, increasing the number of teams, and beginning a review of mission statements, policies, and procedures to ensure congruence with the principles of QI. *Stage 4:* Integrate the QI process into the organization by modifying such processes as resource allocations, job requirements, performance evaluations, strategic planning, and salary administration.

Challenges Ahead

A number of unanswered questions still need to be resolved. The issues still confronting us include evaluation processes, communication systems, employee recognition programs, measurement and benchmarking, just-in-time training on additional tools, and impact on personnel procedures (for example, civil service and union employees).

And there are some other questions. For example, how will the creation and efforts of individual teams merge with the evolution of the organization as a whole? How do we identify and change policies and procedures that run counter to the principles of the QI process? How do we obtain visible signs of commitment from top management? How do we encourage and enhance the respect and trust of our employees? How do we ensure consistent technical and emotional support for team members? And how do we convince top management to be patient? Adopting TQM is no quick fix.

ROBERT S. WINTER *is associate chancellor of the Office of Quality Advancement at the University of Illinois at Chicago.*

Some institutions appoint an individual to provide quality training and coordination.

The Role of the Quality Manager

Nancy Lee Howard

In 1990, the vice president for finance and administration at Oregon State University (OSU) decided to pilot a Total Quality Management (TQM) initiative in administrative areas of the university. The finance and administration division directors served on the steering committee, and the staff development manager provided administrative support. Encouraging early results inspired the university to extend implementation to additional areas.

Like other institutions seriously committed to continuous quality improvement, OSU needed first to define the appropriate level of administrative coordination and support. As implementation expanded, it became apparent that the staff development manager could not fulfill university training needs and provide TQM support at the same time. This prompted the university to establish a six-month administrative fellowship and appoint an individual to work with the staff development manager. The administrative fellowship helped OSU reach conclusions about how a TQM support position should be structured, the responsibilities that it should have, and the value of designating a staff position to support TQM.

At the end of the fellowship, OSU created a permanent position responsible for providing universitywide administrative and technical support for the implementation of TQM. The vice president considered several titles for the position, including *director of quality, quality specialist,* and *quality coordinator.* We selected *quality manager.*

Reporting Structure

We established the quality manager position in the department of human resources. The quality manager has dual reporting responsibility to the director of human resources and the vice president for finance and administration. This arrangement reflects the OSU organizational philosophy, which views quality improvement as one component of a comprehensive approach to human resource management. A close tie exists between quality functions and employee development functions in the areas of team building, facilitation, employee empowerment, organizational development, and problem solving. Working closely within a departmental unit fosters collaboration and encourages the quality manager and the staff development manager to complement each other.

Training

Employee training and development is a critical element in the pursuit of TQM. One of my roles as quality manager is to develop and deliver TQM training.

Anyone considering the development of a training program has a number of options: A turnkey training program can be purchased, consultants can be used to develop and deliver training, staff can be sent to externally sponsored training programs, or training can be developed in-house. We chose to develop training in-house with the aid of a consultant. We had a number of reasons for this decision: It allowed us to retain control of the training curriculum, to design training to fit the institution's culture, and to develop strategies to overcome barriers to the implementation of quality improvement.

A good training process begins with a needs assessment. I worked with the staff development manager, the TQM steering committee, top administration, and employees to identify training needs and desired outcomes. We used the results of this assessment to develop a training program that focuses on leading and facilitating teams. With feedback from participants, we continually improve the training materials and training process.

Training Components

The training program at OSU has four major components: introductory training, strategic planning, team training, and special topics.

Introductory Training. The primary objective of introductory training is to articulate the organization's commitment to TQM. One of the several ways in which management can demonstrate leadership commitment is to be the first to go through the education and training process and then tackle a quality improvement project (Berger, 1991). At OSU, the president, vice presidents, and several other top managers attended an OSU continuing education class taught by Hewlett-Packard TQM staff. The president and vice presidents subsequently formed their own TQM team. OSU then hired a consultant to develop introductory training for pilot team participants (Coate, 1991). Once appointed, the quality manager assumed responsibility for introductory training.

We learned that effective introductory training includes top administration as both participants and presenters. OSU introductory training includes an explanation of the elements of TQM and an illustration of OSU's ten-step TQM process improvement cycle. The desired outcomes are awareness, understanding, and commitment. Initially, we offered a one- to two-hour presentation on an as-requested basis. Now we offer a three-hour introductory session once or twice a month. The audience includes TQM team members and any interested OSU staff.

Strategic Planning. We believe that one critical success factor of our quality improvement initiative is its linkage to strategic planning. Senior management developed a strategic vision to guide the quality initiative, and our strategic plan serves as the foundation for our improvement efforts. We designed a day-and-a-half strategic planning workshop for individual units to develop and refine unit mission and vision statements. The desired outcomes include a clear understanding of the unit's customer expectations, institutional mission and vision, unit mission and vision, and a list of key processes that will serve as the basis for improvement teams.

Team Training. Our approach to process improvement is team based. The heart of our TQM training process is a three-day facilitator and team leader training workshop. The primary objective of team training is to provide participants with the knowledge, skills, and abilities needed to work and communicate in teams. This objective requires the training to provide a detailed explanation of team participant roles and responsibilities, a description of the seven quality tools, and a discussion of team facilitation. Facilitation topics include communication styles, negotiation skills, and consensus building.

Since people learn best by doing, we believe that a successful training program gives participants several opportunities to practice the quality tools and model facilitation skills. The workshop incorporates lecture with discussion and activities. We emphasize experiential learning by using a case study. The workshop is limited to twenty-five participants. Participants work in teams of five to seven, which gives them the opportunity to interact. The audience includes employees who will lead or facilitate a TQM team. The desired outcome is to help teams critically analyze processes, generate creative ideas, and evaluate potential improvements.

Special Topics. As OSU's experience with quality improvement evolves, additional training needs become apparent. We discovered some special topics that require further study. These topics include the cost of quality, benchmarking, maintaining team momentum, advanced statistical process control, and advanced facilitation skills. As the quality manager, I continuously monitor and evaluate training efforts to assure that training needs are being met.

We do not require every employee to be extensively trained before we form the first team. We train leaders and facilitators, who then provide team members with just-in-time training. While it can be argued that all staff should be fully trained before an organization embarks on the TQM journey, few organizations have the resources needed to provide such training. It is also very easy to fall prey to perpetual training without taking any real action. We have demonstrated that teams can achieve successful results with our approach. We recognize that the pursuit of TQM is a long-term commitment. As continuous quality improvement is introduced across campus, OSU staff will continue to be trained immediately before they participate on a team.

Training does require a financial commitment. At OSU, all training is funded by central administration, and participants attend training during regular work hours. To communicate the consistent message that quality improvement is everyone's job and that administration seriously supports the initiative requires thought and attention. For example, what is the message if top managers are provided with lunch for strategic planning sessions while leaders and facilitators must lunch on their own during team training? Our training workshops serve as a model for organizational commitment to the philosophy of continuous quality improvement. We make regular use of participant feedback to improve our training workshops continuously.

Communicating TQM Accomplishments

As the quality manager, I am responsible for communicating team accomplishments to administrators, the campus, and the community. I track team progress, provide guidance and support when necessary, and share results with appropriate audiences. While communication and documentation are necessary, we try to avoid building a paperwork bureaucracy. A quality bureaucracy is the antithesis of continuous quality improvement, so we ask only for necessary information. Communication to administration starts within individual units. Teams report to immediate supervisors weekly, and department managers report monthly. Management communicates to administration quarterly. Team facilitators report team progress to the quality manager on a quarterly basis. To reflect a decentralized, empowered culture, OSU leaves the primary reporting and documentation responsibility at the team level.

Another strategy that we use to provide information about TQM is our annual team fair. The fair is patterned after Xerox Corporation's teamwork celebration. We coordinate an open house once a year at which all teams spend the day sharing their experiences and results with interested visitors.

The quality manager is also called on to share quality improvement success stories with external constituents. The experience of Florida Power and Light, Xerox Corporation, and other award winners shows that requests for information and assistance can be overwhelming. This has certainly been our experience at OSU. Award winners demonstrate that it is vital to maintain a clear focus on one's own organization if one is to continue to thrive with quality management.

Initially, to accommodate requests, we allowed external organizations to send people through our staff training for a fee. Besides satisfying external requests for assistance, this approach helped to fund the cost of our training. However, it was not long before we had more outside requests than we could accommodate. We chose not to displace OSU employees who needed training, so we developed another strategy. Several times a year, we offer a TQM workshop solely for outside participants. This strategy allows us to meet OSU employee training needs and still assist other organizations seeking information about TQM.

Qualifications

As the quality manager, I represent the quality improvement initiative to the rest of the institution and to the outside community. My position requires good oral and written communication skills and good presentation skills. I help teams define the best approach to the process under study, so listening skills and the ability to analyze and synthesize information are also important.

Future

As the quality initiative evolves and grows, it is likely that the role of the quality manager will change. Early in the initiative, I engaged in planning, training, and organizing for quality improvement. As staff become involved and empowered, different demands may arise. Meeting the increasing demands of the entire organization may require a strategy aimed at developing resident experts within divisions or units. As employees become proficient with continuous quality improvement, resident experts will emerge. The quality manager's role then becomes one of working with these experts, who in turn work with teams in their own units. When the initiative matures, my role may become one of monitoring, recognition, and continuous improvement.

Conclusion

Continuous quality improvement is about long-term organizational commitment—commitment to leadership, quality, and change. Every administrative decision communicates this level of commitment. This is especially true when the roles and responsibilities of the individual who will coordinate administration of the quality initiative are defined. While it would be less work to adopt a boilerplate position description, we found that the key to effective TQM is to develop a position aimed at meeting our unique institutional needs in a manner that is consistent with our organizational culture and philosophy.

At OSU, we strive to have all quality initiative decisions convey a consistent message. We know that continuous quality improvement is a never-ending journey and that quality is a moving target. To be effective, the role of the quality manager has to develop, evolve, and change as institutional needs change. Only then can the quality manager guide the institution to successful implementation of TQM.

References

Berger, C. *Quality Improvement Through Leadership and Empowerment: A Business Survival Handbook*. Harrisburg: Pennsylvania MILRITE Council, 1991.

Coate, L. E. "Implementing Total Quality Management in a University Setting." In L. A. Sherr and D. J. Teeter (eds.), *Total Quality Management in Higher Education*. New Directions for Institutional Research, no. 71. San Francisco: Jossey-Bass, 1991.

NANCY LEE HOWARD is the quality manager at Oregon State University, Corvallis.

Preassessment of an issue may help to determine whether a problem warrants a continuous improvement team.

When Is a Problem Not a Problem?

Pam Walter

In the initial implementation of Rio Salado Community College's Total Quality Management (TQM) program, the TQM strategic planning steering team selected processes for improvement from prioritized lists submitted by the nine project identification committees. These committees received recommendations for process improvements from a number of sources, including individual employees, continuous improvement teams, periodic accreditation self-study reports, and analysis of regular surveys of faculty, students, and staff. Although the structure for project selection appeared to be straightforward and objective, several experiences demonstrated flaws in the system.

We selected one project on the basis of a few annoying experiences with the college's voicemail system. The continuous improvement team assigned to improve the process conducted a special survey of all employees to determine the extent of the problem. After reviewing the results, the team determined that the problem was not with the system but with how a few people in the organization were using it. In other words, we were dealing with a people problem, not a process problem. A person from outside of the college met with the team to provide a fresh perspective on the issue. A lack of timely information rather than people or the voicemail system turned out to be the real issue. We are taking steps to correct the real problem.

In another instance, complaints about the college's requisition process led us to appoint a team. The team gathered data revealing that approximately 90 percent of the requisitions are processed smoothly without rework. Most of the problems involved changes in account codes, which the originators of the requisitions could not have foreseen.

We discovered that there is often a great difference between perception and reality when people judge the magnitude of process problems. The

NEW DIRECTIONS FOR INSTITUTIONAL RESEARCH, no. 78, Summer 1993 © Jossey-Bass Publishers

newly created critical process committees are conducting preliminary research to determine the scope and size of the problems presented to them.
If they determine that a process is significant enough to warrant further
study, they designate a continuous improvement team to work on it.

Although the two processes just discussed could be improved, the need
for improvement is minor compared to other processes in the organization,
one of the pitfalls identified in Chapter 24. We anticipate that the critical
process committees will ensure that the time and energies of continuous
improvement teams are focused on areas truly in need of significant improvement and on processes critical to the college.

PAM WALTER is institutional research coordinator at Rio Salado Community
College, Phoenix, Arizona.

Enthusiasm is no substitute for proper training.

Total Quality Management in Word and Deed

Robert A. Yanckello, Thomas B. Flaherty

After reading, discussing, and meeting about Total Quality Management (TQM) for several months, the TQM study group at Central Connecticut State University (CCSU) felt confident enough to initiate a TQM pilot project. After a lengthy brainstorming session, we agreed to examine the freshman mailings process. The senior author agreed to serve as facilitator. Other participants represented the admissions, bursar, financial aid, health services, housing, registrar, and student affairs offices. The group became the freshman mailing committee (FMC), which was chaired by the director of admissions.

At our first meeting, FMC received a brief introduction to TQM, to the purpose of the study group, and to the idea that serving customers is part of our daily work. The group recognized the need for a timetable of what is mailed to freshmen and when it is mailed. As facilitator, I agreed to collect the mailings and develop a flowchart of the freshman mailing process.

At the second meeting of FMC, the group decided to meet once a month for one hour over the next five months. We enlarged the committee to include representatives from each of the four academic schools and the office of public affairs, and membership grew to fifteen people. The focus of subsequent meetings varied widely: We discussed the target population, the definition of quality, and the types of current mailings, and we reviewed many suggestions about how to change what we currently do. There was little or no discussion about defining the problem, collecting data, or testing theories. The group met five times over a period of six months before its members realized that we were functioning much more like a traditional university committee than like a TQM project team. At this point, we thanked the committee for its efforts and killed the pilot project.

Where We Failed

Although the pilot team made an extraordinary effort to examine the freshman mailing process, it is easy in retrospect to identify areas that contributed to its failure:

FMC received an insufficient introduction to the TQM problem-solving approaches, and none of the members had any formal training in TQM.

FMC never developed a proper mission or problem statement.

The facilitator had no formal training in TQM.

The size of the committee (fifteen members) limited its effectiveness even though its members had the necessary training and skills.

The committee met only once a month for one hour—not often enough to make reasonable progress.

Lessons Learned

Solving chronic problems in an organization requires a logical and structured approach making use of data and appropriate tools (Plsek and Onnias, 1989). Lacking the proper training, the TQM study group did not provide FMC with the structure, tools, and resources necessary to carry out a successful TQM project. The lack of proper initial training and the absence of a mission statement contributed to the failure of FMC. Without a framework to guide them or an idea about how to determine what really needed improving, the meetings focused on discussing solutions instead of on identifying the problems that needed improvement.

My lack of knowledge about the quality improvement process only added to FMC's woes. Not understanding how to use the TQM concepts that I read about, I could not guide the team through a structured process. With proper training (as we later found and demonstrated), many mistakes can be avoided, for example, by limiting the size of the team, defining the problem instead of group goals and objectives, having frequent meetings, and functioning as a team with a leader, not as a committee with a chair.

Although some of these mistakes might not seem to be important, they are. By failing to pay attention to these areas, we did the same old thing and achieved the same old results, although we used a different name. We had a large group of people who met once a month for an hour and discussed great ideas for improving a process that it had not documented and that it did not fully understand.

Where Are We Now?

CCSU formed a quality council—the earlier study group—to guide our TQM efforts. There are two project teams operating at this time: the search improvement team and the financial aid consultation team. After carefully documenting and flowcharting the entire sequence of events, the search improvement team is identifying ways to speed up the faculty hiring procedure. The financial aid consultation team is in the diagnostic phase of its project, developing a flowchart of the process. Moving slowly, and with the help of the Juran Institute, we are making excellent progress since our original debacle.

Reference

Plsek, P. E., and Onnias, A. *Juran Institute Quality Improvement Tools: Problem Solving Glossary.* Wilton, Conn.: Juran Institute, 1989.

ROBERT A. YANCKELLO *is assistant director of planning at Central Connecticut State University, New Britain.*

THOMAS B. FLAHERTY *is director of planning at Central Connecticut State University.*

A team designing a Total Quality Management effort during a time of administrative reorganization sees its recommendations for implementation put on hold.

A Quality Initiative Postponed

Jeffrey D. Liebmann

In 1990, the administrative organization at the University of Pittsburgh was in turmoil. The president, a nationally recognized figure, was the longest-term head of a major college or university at that time. However, several events led to a faculty vote of no confidence and to a decline in campus morale. By late 1990, the president and several high-level administrators had either left the university or announced their retirement. Dissatisfaction with the administration and decision-making processes was widespread.

Across the campus, administrators tried to deal with the growing climate of distrust and uncertainty. Administrators were faced with the problems associated with finishing a troubled presidency as well as with laying the groundwork for the entrance of new institutional leadership. At that time, the vice president for administration managed thirteen units with nearly twelve hundred employees. He named one of his unit heads to the position of quality director and charged him with leading a Total Quality Management (TQM) effort in the Office of Administration. He later called the effort People Achieving Quality (PAQ).

The PAQ quality leadership committee consisted of the vice president and his unit heads. Their role included implementing and administering PAQ and writing vision and mission statements. The quality design team, which served as the primary planning and development group, consisted of selected middle management individuals from each unit. The design team's objectives included the following: developing a strategy to implement a quality process in the office of administration, providing direction and guidance for implementation, and adjusting the process to meet changing organizational needs. The proposed plan also called for establishing quality lead teams, including each unit's head and selected managers, to write the unit mission and administer assessment, evaluation, and rewards and recognition efforts within the unit; quality facilitators trained to act as internal consultants on problem definition, team building, and TQM concepts; and quality improvement teams to examine processes and recommend changes.

Chronology of Events

Between January and April 1991, the quality director and his two-person quality implementation working committee chose an organizational structure, training materials, consultants, and quality design team. In May, the quality design team met for the first time. It was introduced to TQM theory at this meeting. Between June and August, the design team met twice each week. The president retired, and his successor took office. In September, the design team presented a sixteen-month implementation plan proposing an extensive awareness campaign coupled with communication efforts and training programs for unit heads, more than two hundred supervisors, and more than nine hundred nonsupervisory staff. In October, the vice president told the design team that the new interim senior vice presidents were putting the quality effort on hold and that the design team would meet no longer. An administrative reorganization eliminated the vice president's position. Support for continuing PAQ, including all financial commitments for training, quickly disappeared. The quality director returned to his administrative position.

As a member of the design team, I was very skeptical after my first exposure to TQM and the proposed draft quality organizational structure. I based my skepticism on some philosophical differences with TQM itself as well as on doubts concerning the institution's motivations for implementing it. Members of the design team spent many hours debating the team's true function and the level of authority that it would have in the process. However, the basic TQM theories did seem sound. I and others slowly began to believe that TQM had something to offer the University of Pittsburgh, even during this tumultuous time.

Throughout the summer, the design team debated and engaged in soul-searching but slowly began to feel ownership of the PAQ design process. After hundreds of hours of effort, we received a positive but unenthusiastic response from upper management. One design team member felt that the leadership committee appreciated the amount of effort put into our plan but not its content. The vice president did not formally approve our plan, nor did he provide significant feedback about the presentation.

Problems

A variety of factors contributed to the failure of the PAQ effort. While concerns with the application of TQM theory and philosophy contributed to some degree, most factors involved the organization of the PAQ process, particularly the definition and use of the quality design team.

Flaws in Organizational Structure. The PAQ structure placed the design team in line between the unit lead teams and the quality leadership committee. Yet, many members of the design team believed that the group operated on the sidelines in an advisory, not an implementing, capacity. The leadership committee charged us to design a process to empower employees, but it did not empower the team. In fact, process design flaws, poor execution, and circumstances at the institution prevented achievement of PAQ's lofty goals.

Insufficient Communication. The design team had no formal vehicle and almost no opportunities for direct contact with the vice president or the quality leadership committee. This created much frustration when the vice president and the leadership committee, through the quality director and the quality implementation working committee, seemed unreceptive toward the ideas and initiatives that the design team was articulating.

Hidden Agendas. The design team agonized over recommendations only to see them rejected with no recognition of their rationale. In the words of one design team member, it seemed as though there were an unrevealed PAQ master plan. (Another team member called it the "blueprint.") When the design team questioned basic assumptions or discussed taking PAQ in directions at variance with the master plan, it met with great resistance from the quality director and the quality implementation working committee.

Deteriorating Relationships. The relationship between the quality director and the quality design team deteriorated tremendously between June and September. In addition to some differences in fundamental TQM philosophy, many members believed that the quality director did not present design team recommendations to the vice president or leadership committee accurately. Some believed that he openly disregarded the consensus of the design team. As a result of this absence of clear and open dialogue between PAQ entities, the quality director lost the trust of many design team members.

Limited Resources. Having only one master certified trainer left the process vulnerable. After committing time and money obtaining master certification from the provider of the training materials for the director of employee development, the employee left the university. Because of the time involved in master certification, scheduling was set back by several months.

Limited Commitment. Some unit heads openly supported the process, while others were indifferent. Some unit heads resisted releasing their staff to the frequent design team meetings, and few members attended every meeting. Throughout the process, several design team members believed that commitment to PAQ would weaken when plans called for significant funding and staff release time.

Weak Support. Support from leadership was strong verbally but weak in actions. Leaders made careless remarks that eroded the trust and commitment that had taken months to engender. The vice president, quality director, and quality implementation working committee discussed TQM concepts articulately, but they often did not practice TQM methods in day-to-day activities.

Political Pressures. The design team was often unable to focus solely on quality issues. From 1989 to 1991, the university's president and administration were under intense pressure from campus constituencies, state government, and local media. The environment on campus was hostile and tense. Whatever the actual intent of the PAQ initiative, it was difficult for design team members to eliminate politics from implementation and to believe that the motives for initiating quality on campus were sincere.

Despite these problems, the design team did some incredible work. Before the collapse of the effort in October, even the most skeptical members of the design team accepted many TQM concepts. Members wanted to implement PAQ and spread the quality word to others. The design team initiated a passive awareness campaign, made final plans for presentations to all supervisory staff, and started making initial assignments for managerial training. The implementation plan also proposed establishing subgroups to examine issues related to rewards and recognition, to draft and design brochures and newsletters, and to promote overall awareness of the effort.

In the end, however, the commitment of design team members to TQM deteriorated as a result of these problems and strengthened suspicions that politics and hidden agendas influenced PAQ design and purpose. The design team lost confidence in its ability to implement recommendations effectively. Miscommunication and lack of support convinced the design team that its efforts to promote the quality effort were not truly a high priority.

These middle managers fought through much doubt and criticism to accept the tenets of TQM. In the end, failure of the process to approve and implement design team recommendations and the inability of upper management to support the design team's work left its members feeling abandoned.

Lessons Learned

The experience at the University of Pittsburgh suggests some valuable lessons for those pursuing TQM. First, without total commitment to TQM from some level of management, the effort faces difficult odds. Whether the commitment to quality and leading by example comes from a president, vice president, or director, it must be strong and visible. Without such leadership, one cannot get employees to commit to increased productivity and imagination.

Second, quality is not something that one can do in addition to ongoing tasks. It has to take top priority. If one must delay a project or responsibility during implementation, then so be it. Employees will not appreciate the importance of quality if it does not carry real weight in their own work assignments.

Third, do not wait until the wolf is at the door. During a crisis, turf battles, distractions, and tension will keep people from adapting to a quality management style.

Fourth, make participation and communication as open as possible. Often, employees are skeptical not of quality concepts but of the institution's commitment to empower people.

Fifth, and probably most important, articulate the parameters of the quality process carefully and completely. Leave absolutely no doubt as to the roles and responsibilities of the teams in the process. Then act in a manner consistent with those parameters.

In spite of the many obstacles that eventually ended the University of Pittsburgh's initial attempt at TQM, the design team's proposal process remains feasible. Certainly, design team members retain some of the TQM principles in spite of the manner in which their participation in this effort ended. Quality process implementation at Pittsburgh may yet occur through smaller efforts spearheaded by the Office of Human Resources. A new supervisory training program scheduled for full implementation in 1993 includes an introduction to TQM principles. Another initiative, a continuous improvement process, is scheduled for implementation over the next five years. After being tested in the Office of Human Resources, the process is expected to grow gradually in carefully selected areas. Members of the original PAQ quality design team have little involvement in these efforts.

JEFFREY D. LIEBMANN is manager of strategic planning in the Office of Budget, Planning, and Analysis at the University of Pittsburgh.

Tools alone will not produce desired changes if we do not also account for variation among team members' management styles.

Confluence Between Standard Operating Paradigms and Total Quality Management

Valerie J. Broughton

One major focus of the institutional research office (IR) at the University of Minnesota–Duluth (UMD) is to prepare information and analyses concerning academic programs. In particular, the office of the vice chancellor for academic affairs depends on IR to provide quantitative analyses, ratios, and other cost-benefit data for the making of resource allocation decisions. Resource decisions also consider information on program plans, quality, future potential, and overall contribution to the campus mission.

For a number of years, there have been annual discussions of the measurement criteria used in decision making, and each time the deliberations ended unsuccessfully. The dialogue wandered, no agreements were reached, and conflict over the data that should be used to inform decisions continued. To address this friction, the Council of Deans and Academic Administrators (CODAA) devoted the majority of its spring 1992 retreat to the issue of data use in decision making and the development of definitions and analyses for future use.

IR had no emotional ties to existing definitions, and it viewed the retreat as a welcome process improvement exercise. CODAA hoped to use Total Quality Management (TQM) tools to reach agreement on definitions. CODAA members had participated in many TQM training sessions conducted by external consultants, and they had learned both problem-solving and strategic management tools. The TQM training included use of flip charts for documenting outcomes and yellow sticky pads to facilitate brainstorming. Charts and sticky pads were in plentiful supply at the off-campus conference facility that served as the retreat site. We invited the vice chancellor for finance and operations, a well-respected colleague neutral on this issue, to serve as facilitator.

The process began by having participants list data topics of concern. They wrote the descriptive phrases on sticky pads and grouped the items into major topics. The group tried to sequence discussion topics, but group members could not agree. Uncertainty about what TQM tool to use surfaced, and the process began to disintegrate. The TQM purists in the group insisted that we start with the item likely to have the biggest impact if it was improved. Other experienced campus administrators "knew" which concerns had been around the longest and accordingly were the most important. By majority rule, we selected the first topic. Discussion wandered into the second topic, generating new issues to add to the original list. During the debate, participants focused on the same "pet peeve" topics that had been brought up in the traditional sessions that had taken place every spring.

In the end, we did not establish any new or revised measures, but one unanticipated outcome occurred. Several participants observed that the issue of data elements seemed secondary to the process by which we make decisions. That is, the root cause of the concerns about data utilization in resource allocation is not the numbers, their origin, or the methods that we use to transform and compare them but rather the data that are used for particular decisions. Prompted by these comments, the vice chancellor for academic administration explained the process that she uses for making decisions, described why empirical indicators are helpful, and then answered questions.

Problems Confronted

The case just outlined shows how the use of TQM tools can help an organization to move forward. A breakthrough occurred when we hypothesized and addressed a root cause, that is, when we knew what data are used for which decisions. But we may have defined the retreat topic too loosely to yield decisive results. The issue may have been too large. Often, we tackle large obstacles, discuss what we think are the causes, evaluate potential solutions, and then plan. Normally, administrators spend little time defining problems. TQM tools may be more helpful when we define issues clearly and narrowly.

TQM implores us to be patient. We expected fifteen administrators to solve a years-old nagging problem during two four-hour sessions. What optimism! We approached the problem as a strategic management issue rather than as a routine management problem. Perhaps we selected the wrong approach and tools in light of the constraints on meeting time. Moreover, while many participants had TQM training, most had not actually used its tools. Perhaps the knowledge, attitudes, and approaches to problem solving in general and to TQM in particular varied too widely for the group to function successfully as a TQM team.

Observations About Team Member Characteristics

Group or team members typically vary along several dimensions: TQM purist versus improved management techniques, impatient versus patient, tolerance of ambiguity versus fear of failure, and talkers versus doers. There are no inherently positive or negative values in these seemingly opposing dimensions. However, the capacity of a team to accommodate these diverse attitudes can influence the likelihood that a TQM process will succeed. For example, a TQM purist might read Deming's (1986) *Out of the Crisis* and believe that no compromises are possible when continuous improvement methodologies are implemented. The improver believes that some TQM tools might be helpful but that the tools are not really new and that good management depends on style and leadership.

In the long run, patience might be the most important characteristic for an organization to possess if TQM practices are to take hold. Patient administrators who foster development of TQM principles while being held accountable for current outcomes face a dilemma: Which comes first, the organization developing tolerance for long-term approaches or leaders within the organization allowing process improvement developments? This may not be an either-or situation. The institution may move modestly as a few units develop long-term improvement strategies and through their successes influence additional unit leaders to become more patient and accepting of long-term improvements.

Most of us in higher education consider ourselves successful in what we do. In pursuing TQM, we take chances that might lead to failure if failure is defined as implementing a solution that does not have the desired effect. The plan-do-check-act cycle implies that solutions require systematic monitoring, adjustment, and revision. TQM teaches us that with careful thought, analysis, and planning our solutions will be successful.

Finally, there is the spectrum from action-oriented team members to team members who always need more analyses. TQM practice encourages the doer to allow time for careful consideration and discovery of root causes and prods the analytical deliberator to agree to act as part of the plan-do-check-act cycle. Again, it is not an either-or question but rather one of achieving a balance between analysis and action.

The CODAA retreat designed to improve the data used in resource allocation considerations included people trained in TQM ideals, purposes, tools, and techniques. These people also act in accordance with their own individual models of successful operation. The intersection of those two phenomena created an atmosphere that led to a breakthrough in understanding differences between the quality of the data and how the data are used for making decisions.

Reference

Deming, W. E. *Out of the Crisis*. Cambridge: Center for Advanced Engineering Study, Massachusetts Institute of Technology, 1986.

VALERIE J. BROUGHTON is associate vice chancellor for academic affairs at the University of Minnesota, Duluth.

Experiences in the corporate sector demonstrate that there are many recipes for disaster with Total Quality Management.

The Challenge:
Overcoming the Pitfalls

G. Gregory Lozier, Deborah J. Teeter

In his keynote address at Quality Forum VIII, Edwin Artzt, chairman and chief executive of the Procter and Gamble Company, observed that "one of the key business challenges of the 1990s [is] meeting consumers' increasing demand for value" (Artzt, 1992). The means of meeting this challenge, according to Artzt, is total quality.

Higher education consumers—students, parents, taxpayers, governments, and industry—are also increasing their demands for value. Articles on higher education frequently comment on the growing concerns about productivity, escalating tuition, reduced public confidence, renewed calls for accountability, and perceived declines in quality. The vignettes in this volume attest the commitment that many colleges and universities are making to Total Quality Management (TQM), or Continuous Quality Improvement, to address these critical concerns. But is TQM all that some make it out to be?

Corporate Status

Several articles in the popular press in 1992 suggest that the corporate world is souring on TQM. The theme of these articles is that business and industry report little payoff from TQM, including a lack of protection from hard times: A study of thirty quality programs by the McKinsey Consulting Group in Boston concludes that two-thirds of the programs had stalled or failed to produce anticipated real improvements ("Quality Programs Show Shoddy Results," 1992). A survey by Arthur D. Little of five hundred firms reports that only 36 percent indicated that TQM was having a significant impact and providing overall improved competitiveness ("The Cost of Quality," 1992; "Special Report: Quality," 1992; "Making Quality More Than a Fad," 1992). The Rath and Strong consulting firm survey of senior managers at ninety-five corporations reports that only 26 percent of these managers gave TQM a grade of A or B, whereas over 50 percent gave grades of D and F, regarding TQM's ability to improve market share, rein in costs, and make customers happy ("The Cost of Quality," 1992; "Special Report: Quality," 1992; "Making Quality More Than a Fad," 1992). A survey by the American Electronics Association of three hundred electronics companies reports that among 73 percent of the firms with total quality programs underway, 63 percent indicated that the programs had failed to improve quality defects by even as much as 10 percent (Schaffer and Thomson, 1992).

However, the rush to criticize the quality movement comes about not only because of such studies but also, according to a number of chief executives, because quality is making more news: " 'More awareness means more rebuttals' " ("Speaking of Quality," 1993, p. 3). Furthermore, not all studies are negative. A 1989 Gallup survey of corporate executives for the American Society for Quality Control reports that "the quality leader in any industry is less susceptible to the effects of recession" (Caine, 1992, p. 1). And a study by the U.S. General Accounting Office of twenty Baldrige award nominees for corporate quality achievements reports that companies using TQM practices *properly designed and implemented* achieved improvements in employee relations, operating procedures, customer satisfaction, and financial performance (U.S. General Accounting Office, 1991).

Considering higher education's reluctance to adopt practices and terminologies from business, should colleges and universities be scrambling to learn more about TQM? Or, can higher education institutions, using the tools of scholarship to learn systematically from both successes and failures, become proactive participants in the evolution of TQM? Increasingly, a literature is evolving that analyzes the successes and failures of TQM and offers a summary of the pitfalls and flaws of TQM practices in companies reporting minimal or no positive results (Bailey and others, 1993; Chang, 1993; Fife, 1992; Leibmann, 1992; McLagan, 1991; Schaffer and Thomson, 1992; Schmidt and Finnigan, 1992). These analyses indicate that the problem is not with the quality concepts but rather with the practices of these companies. A synthesis of these analyses follows here.

Reliance on Packaged TQM Programs

Too many corporations take an off-the-shelf TQM formula and impose it on their employees without regard to differences among organizations or in the environments in which they function. Dedication to following the steps of standardized programs that are inimical to an organization's culture is likely to lead to frustration and only limited, marginal results in continuous improvement. The pursuit of quality requires thoughtful planning and a strategy that meets the particular needs of the organization. As Ricklefs (1992) has observed, "There are no cookbooks. You and your institution's leadership need to develop your own quality improvement strategy."

Large-Scale, Diffuse Implementation

In their frenzy to improve quality, many corporations generate too much activity too soon. Rather than develop a thoughtful strategy, the TQM process becomes the end rather than the means. Such organizations typically experience team overkill, mistakenly measure success by the number of teams or the number of employees involved, and experience only minimal or fleeting improvements. In contrast, real, lasting results can be achieved when improvement is "viewed as a continuum—a need to walk before running or to master algebra before tackling calculus" (Ernst and Young and American Quality Foundation, 1992, p. 7). Such a studied approach to TQM is less likely to expend substantial energy and resources for limited or no results.

Mass Training Programs

The development of comprehensive, unfocused training programs is usually highly correlated with large-scale, diffuse implementation. Again, success is measured by the number of employees trained rather than by any particular qualitative results. In contrast to just-in-time training, these comprehensive training programs often do not sufficiently inform employees about the overall strategy and goals of the quality effort and fail to provide adequate support systems. Rather, the focus is on training in tools and process improvement, and the need for education about the quality strategy is slighted or ignored altogether.

Measurement Paralysis

Measurement paralysis is not unique to TQM. Lacking explicit goals for TQM, teams engage in a flurry of data collection activities resulting in too much data, measure the wrong things, and inadequately analyze the data. Measurement is a critical aspect of TQM, but the focus should be on data to improve processes, not just on activity levels.

Overemphasis on TQM Tools

The tools of TQM are extremely powerful when used as the means to improve a well-defined, strategically based TQM process. However, caught up in the ritual of TQM, some corporations find that they spend a great deal of energy going through the motions, without realizing much subsequent benefit. Team members become preoccupied with drawing the perfect flowchart or cause-and-effect diagram, without much awareness of the appropriate use of such tools. Teams fail to recognize that the tools are a means to process improvement and not an end in themselves. This problem frequently is confronted by organizations that adopt a standardized, lockstep TQM program in which tool A is always used when performing step 1.

Process Selection Issues

Many corporations are focusing their TQM efforts on trivial processes, unrelated to the major issues and strategies of the organizations. Although such activities can result in process improvements that do in fact generate increased customer satisfaction, they are not likely to contribute significantly to the overall competitiveness and profitability of an organization. Typically, firms in this situation have not systematically asked and answered such questions as: What are the criteria for picking a process to target for improvement? Who can pick? What processes are most critical to the achievement of the organization's strategic goals?

Outmoded Reward Structures

Traditional reward systems are based on the appraisal of the individual. Rather than contribute to improved performance, annual reviews, performance rankings, and merit pay systems typically serve to elevate staff fear and anxiety. When many corporations adopted what they thought was TQM, few scrapped their existing evaluation and reward systems, failing to take into account the critical role that team problem solving plays in continuous improvement. Stuck with conventional incentive programs, individuals working on process improvement teams continue to be more concerned with personally pleasing the supervisor than with pursuing quality improvement.

Simplistic Views of Change and Cultural Transformation

TQM requires us to make fundamental changes in the way in which we think about our organizations. This cultural transformation cannot be achieved with a little fix here and a small improvement there. Corporations that have achieved little success with TQM have suffered from some or all of the following attributes: lack of management commitment, failure to understand the extended time frame needed to bring about broadscale change, discontinuity of the effort, and inability to make TQM routine, an integral part of the day-to-day operations. As Pifer (Schmidt and Finnigan, 1992, p. 336) has observed, the result is employee confusion: " 'Why are we doing this, *really*?' "

Why? The answer is usually attributable to a leader's commitment to quality improvement and a desire to transform the organization. The chief executive officer of one corporation is reported to have observed, when asked about the status of TQM in his organization, "We about stopped, but gave it one more try." And to make that effort, they turned to the principles of TQM and looked for the root causes in their TQM process that were thwarting their efforts. They realized that it was not the philosophy of TQM that was failing but rather the effort.

How are the efforts in colleges and universities faring? The vignettes in this volume provide rich examples of diverse approaches to the pursuit of quality. Some institutions are experiencing considerable success and report significant improvements in results. Others have met resistance, or they have redirected their efforts, or they are still virtually in the starting blocks. Most colleges and universities are still in the bleachers and are not yet ready to try out the new equipment. Ultimately, the path to quality is an appropriate blend of strategic planning, education and training, practicing, achieving results, and rewarding personnel.

References

Artzt, E. L. "Redefining Quality: The New Relationship Between Quality, Price and Value." Keynote address presented at Quality Forum VIII, New York, October 1992.

Bailey, M., and others. "Recipes for Disaster." *Quality Progress*, 1993, 26 (1), 55–58.

Caine, R. "Quality Critical in Turning the Economy Around." *On Q: The Official Newsletter of the American Society for Quality Control*, 1992, 7 (4), 1–2.

Chang, R. Y. "When TQM Goes Nowhere." *Training and Development*, 1993, 47 (1), 22–29.

"The Cost of Quality." *Newsweek*, Sept. 7, 1992, pp. 48–49.

Ernst and Young and American Quality Foundation. *Best Practices Report: An Analysis of Management Practices That Impact Performance*. Milwaukee, Wis.: American Society for Quality Control, 1992.

Fife, S. "The Total Quality Muddle." *Report on Business*, 1992, 9 (5), 64–73.

Leibman, M. S. "Getting Results from TQM." *HR Magazine*, 1992, 37 (9), 34–38.

McLagan, P. "The Dark Side of Quality." *Training*, 1991, 28 (11), 31–33.

"Making Quality More Than a Fad." *Fortune*, May 18, 1992, pp. 12–13.

On Q, 1992, 7 (4).

On Q, 1993, 8 (1).

"Quality Programs Show Shoddy Results." *Wall Street Journal*, May 14, 1992, pp. B1, B7.

Ricklefs, M. J. "Total Quality Management in the Academic and Business Life of a University." Workshop presented at the symposium Quality in Action in Academia, Lehigh Valley, Pennsylvania, July 1992.

Schaffer, R. H., and Thomson, H. A. "Successful Change Programs Begin with Results." *Harvard Business Review*, 1992, 70 (1), 80–89.

Schmidt, W. H., and Finnigan, J. P. *The Race Without a Finish Line: America's Quest for Total Quality*. San Francisco: Jossey-Bass, 1992.

"Speaking of Quality." *On Q: The Official Newsletter of the American Society for Quality Control*, 1993, 8 (1), 3.

"Special Report: Quality." *Business Week*, Nov. 30, 1992, pp. 66–74.

U.S. General Accounting Office. *Management Practices: U.S. Companies Improve Performance Through Quality Efforts*. GAO/NSIAD-91-190. Washington, D.C.: Government Printing Office, 1991.

G. GREGORY LOZIER is executive director of planning and analysis and a member of the graduate faculty in higher education at The Pennsylvania State University.

DEBORAH J. TEETER is director of institutional research and planning at The University of Kansas, Lawrence.

APPENDIX

Total Quality Management Status of Represented Institutions

A. Institutional Characteristics

Institution	Type	Affiliation/ Control	Fall 1992 Head Count
Central Connecticut State University	Comprehensive	State	13,784
Delaware County Community College	Two year	State/local	10,269
Fox Valley Technical College	Two year	State/local	5,000
Oregon State University	Doctoral	State	14,336
Pennsylvania State University	Doctoral	State-related	70,576
Rio Salado Community College	Two year	State/local	12,800
Samford University	Doctoral	Southern Baptist	4,341
University of Amsterdam	Doctoral	National	30,000
University of Kansas-Lawrence	Doctoral	State	26,465
University of Illinois-Chicago	Doctoral	State	24,985
University of Miami	Doctoral	Independent	14,155
University of Minnesota-Duluth	Comprehensive	State	7,680
University of Pennsylvania	Doctoral	Independent	22,315
University of Pittsburgh	Doctoral	State-related	34,242
University of Rhode Island	Doctoral	State	15,451

B. Total Quality Management Status

Institution	Terminology	Year Introduced/ Initiated	Champion	Current Organizational Structure		
				Management Team (Name)	New, Existing, Modified	Quality Coordinator (Title)
Central Connecticut State University	Quality Improvement Process	1989	President	Quality Council	Modified	
Delaware County Community College	Total Quality Management	1985	President	Total Quality Steering Group	New	Quality coordinator (full-time)
Fox Valley Technical College		1985	President	Total Quality Leadership Team	Modified	Quality coordinator (full-time)
Oregon State University	Total Quality Management	1989	President and vice president-administration			Quality manager (full-time)
Pennsylvania State University	Continuous Quality Improvement (CQI)	1991	Executive vice president/provost	University Council on CQI	New	Director of Continuous Quality Improvement (full-time)
Rio Salado Community College	Total Quality Management	1991	President	Strategic Planning Steering Team		Total Quality Management coordinator (add-on responsibility)
Samford University	Student–First Quality Quest	1989	President	President's Quality Council		Assistant to the provost for quality assessment (part-time)

University	Program	Year	Executive	Team/Committee	Status	Quality Role
University of Amsterdam	Quality of Education—Improvement of Teaching-Learning	1991	Executive board	Educational Quality Project Team	New	Quality manager (full-time)
University of Kansas-Lawrence		1991	Associate vice chancellor-administration and finance	Ad Hoc TQM Group	New	
University of Illinois-Chicago	Quality Advancement	1991	Chancellor			Associate chancellor for quality advancement (full-time)
University of Miami		1989	Senior vice president-business and finance	Customer Satisfaction Team		Associate treasurer (add-on responsibility)
University of Minnesota-Duluth		1989	Vice chancellor-academic support and student life			
University of Pennsylvania	Total Quality Management	1990	Executive vice president	Quality Council	Modified	Quality consultant (add-on responsibility)
University of Pittsburgh	People Achieving Quality	1991	Vice president-administration	Quality Leadership Committee	New	Quality director (add-on responsibility)
University of Rhode Island		1991	President			

B. Total Quality Management Status *(continued)*

	Why the Pursuit?			
	External	Internal	Extent of the Pursuit	Corporate Partner/Consultant
Central Connecticut State University	Corporate urging Alumni urging	Fiscal concerns Administrative concerns Improve quality	Institution-wide	Juran Institute
Delaware County Community College		Fiscal concerns/leverage limited resources Enhance planning Improve quality	Institution-wide	None
Fox Valley Technical College	Corporate urging	Presidential philosophy Improve quality Improve organizational climate	Institution-wide	None
Oregon State University	Corporate urging Alumni urging	Presidential philosophy Enhance productivity Fiscal concerns Administrative concerns Improve quality Improve service to customers	Institution-wide	IBM/Xerox
Pennsylvania State University	Corporate urging	Provost philosophy Enhance productivity Enhance planning Improve quality "Practice What We Teach" Tied to assessment	Institution-wide—initial focus in support areas	DuPont
Rio Salado Community College		Enhance productivity Enhance planning Improve quality	Institution-wide	Technology Exchange Center

Institution	External pressure	Reasons/Impetus	Scope	Consultants
Samford University		Presidential philosophy Enhance planning Tied to assessment	Institution-wide	Casey Collett, Joann DeMott, David Sylwester
University of Amsterdam	Public accountability State mandate	Executive board philosophy Enhance productivity Improve quality Tied to assessment	Academic departments	None
University of Kansas-Lawrence		Enhance productivity Administrative concerns Improve quality	Administrative support services	None
University of Illinois-Chicago		Chancellor's philosophy Administrative concerns Improve quality	Institution-wide	None
University of Miami		Senior vice president's philosophy Improve quality Improve service to students and others	Business and finance	None
University of Minnesota-Duluth		Improve quality	Institution-wide	IBM–Rochester Casey Collett
University of Pennsylvania		Enhance productivity Enhance planning Improve quality	Administration and some academic units	Juran Institute GOAL/QPC
University of Pittsburgh		Enhance productivity Fiscal concerns Administrative concerns Improve quality	Administration	None
University of Rhode Island		Presidential philosophy Enhance productivity Fiscal concerns	Institution-wide—primarily administration and student services	PPG

B. Total Quality Management Status *(continued)*

Initial Pursuit Strategy (represents situation at onset rather than current practice)

Institution	Implementation (Top Down, Bottom Up, Mixed)	Education/Training	Level of Communication	Rewards/Recognition Program	Role of Institutional Research/Planning
Central Connecticut State University	Top down	External consultants	Moderate exposure	Under review	Represented on design/management team Team facilitator
Delaware County Community College	Top down	External consultants Internally developed training	Moderate exposure	Under review	Represented on design/management team Data providers Part of training team Conduct customer research Assist staff
Fox Valley Technical College	Top down	Internally developed training	High profile	Formal and informal	Data providers Conduct customer research Focus group facilitator
Oregon State University	Top down	External consultants	Moderate exposure	Under review	Data providers Team facilitator
Pennsylvania State University	Mixed	External consultants	Moderate exposure	Under review	Represented on design/management team Data providers Part of training team Team facilitator
Rio Salado Community College	Mixed	External consultants	High profile	Formal	Represented on design/management team Data providers Part of training team Conduct customer research Team facilitator

Institution	Direction	Training approach	Profile	Status	Role
Samford University	Top down	External consultants / Internally developed training	High profile	Informal	Data providers / Assist staff
University of Amsterdam	Mixed	Internally developed training	High profile	Under review	Data providers / Conduct customer research
University of Kansas-Lawrence	Mixed	External consultants		Under review	Represented on design/ management team / Data providers / Part of training team / Team facilitator
University of Illinois-Chicago	Mixed	External consultants / Internally developed training	Moderate exposure	Under review	Data providers
University of Miami	Top down within business and finance	Internally developed training	Moderate exposure within business and finance	Under review	Represented on design/ management team / Conduct customer research
University of Minnesota-Duluth	Top down	External consultants	Moderate exposure		Represented on design/ management team / Data providers / Conduct customer research
University of Pennsylvania	Top down	External consultants	Moderate exposure	Formal	No official role
University of Pittsburgh	Top down	Internally developed training using Zenger-Miller materials	High profile	Formal	Represented on design/ management team / Part of training team / Team facilitator
University of Rhode Island	Top down	External consultants	High profile	Formal	Data providers

INDEX

ORDERING INFORMATION

NEW DIRECTIONS FOR INSTITUTIONAL RESEARCH is a series of paperback books that provides planners and administrators in all types of academic institutions with guidelines in such areas as resource coordination, information analysis, program evaluation, and institutional management. Books in the series are published quarterly in Spring, Summer, Fall, and Winter and are available for purchase by subscription as well as by single copy.

SUBSCRIPTIONS for 1993 cost $45.00 for individuals (a savings of 20 percent over single-copy prices) and $60.00 for institutions, agencies, and libraries. Please do not send institutional checks for personal subscriptions. Standing orders are accepted.

SINGLE COPIES cost $14.95 when payment accompanies order. (California, New Jersey, New York, and Washington, D.C., residents please include appropriate sales tax.) Billed orders will be charged postage and handling.

DISCOUNTS FOR QUANTITY ORDERS are available. Please write to the address below for information.

ALL ORDERS must include either the name of an individual or an official purchase order number. Please submit your order as follows:
  Subscriptions: specify series and year subscription is to begin
  Single copies: include individual title code (such as IR1)

MAIL ALL U.S. ORDERS TO:
  Jossey-Bass Publishers
  350 Sansome Street
  San Francisco, CA 94104

FOR SINGLE-COPY SALES OUTSIDE OF THE UNITED STATES CONTACT:
  Maxwell Macmillan International Publishing Group
  866 Third Avenue
  New York, NY 10022

FOR SUBSCRIPTION SALES OUTSIDE OF THE UNITED STATES, contact
  any international subscription agency, or Jossey-Bass directly.